THE
Appalachian Trail
CELEBRATING AMERICA'S HIKING TRAIL

FOREWORD BY

BILL BRYSON

TO THE FOUR GENERATIONS OF VOLUNTEERS AND ON-THE-GROUND AGENCY PARTNERS

WHO CREATED THE APPALACHIAN TRAIL

AND HAVE KEPT IT BLOOMING EVER SINCE.

Contents

Foreword

By **BILL BRYSON**

Author of *A Walk in the Woods: Rediscovering America on the Appalachian Trail*

I DON'T KNOW WHEN I FIRST HEARD OF THE APPALACHIAN TRAIL, BUT I REMEMBER very clearly when I first saw it. I had just moved back to the United States from England, where I had lived for the previous 18 years, and was out for an exploratory walk around my new town of Hanover, New Hampshire, when I came upon an opening into some woods on the edge of town where a well-groomed path wound off into the trees.

Beside the path was a signboard announcing that this was the famous Appalachian Trail. A distance guide informed me that if I followed the Trail north from here it would take me over the White Mountains all the way to Katahdin in Maine, not far short of the Canadian border, some 442 miles away. If I turned in the other direction, I could walk 1,742 miles to the green mountains of Georgia through some of the most glorious landscapes of the eastern United States, along the spine of this most ancient and storied chain of mountains.

Even now I can't entirely account for it, but there was something so beguiling about that trail disappearing into the woods, and something so preposterously challenging about those unimaginable distances, that I decided more or less there and then to try to do it. I would hike the Appalachian Trail from end to end, and in so doing I would rediscover, in a satisfyingly elemental way, the country that I had left as a young man and was now returning to in middle age.

An old friend named Stephen Katz decided to join me, adding both welcome companionship and bonus levels of challenge to the enterprise. And so one frosty late-winter morning in 1996, we set off up Springer Mountain in Georgia on what would easily be the most challenging adventure of our lives, and the best.

Very quickly we learned, as thousands had before us and as this splendid volume makes manifestly clear, that the Appalachian Trail is a whole lot more than just a trail. It is a haven, a time capsule, a spirited community, a laboratory, a whole spectrum of ecosystems, a living museum, an economic entity, a park, an assault course, a great secret, a kind of miracle. It is, in short, a place like no other.

There is only one rule of admission: you must come on foot. And what a difference that makes. I have to say that hiking the Appalachian Trail—or, to put it rather more accurately in our case, failing to hike the Appalachian Trail, but failing gamely—was the hardest thing that either of us had ever attempted to do. I can unhesitatingly say that I have never been so tired and wet and cold and stiff and bedraggled as I often was along the A.T.—and for Katz you may double those qualities

and add several additional ones. But I have also never, anywhere, experienced more transcendently sublime moments than I did in our long summer of toiling up and down mountains.

I wasn't always aware of it at the time, but in retrospect there were certain things that we got from the Trail—that I think nearly everyone gets from the Trail—that we could never have found without going through the effort and deprivation of a long hike through the wilderness.

The first was the discovery that the world is a really big place. You cannot believe how big the world truly is until you take it on, on foot. One of the minor tragedies of the age in which we live is that we have lost nearly all our sense of scale. We perceive the world these days almost exclusively in terms of vehicular distance. If I ask you to try to imagine the 2,200 miles of the Appalachian Trail, you'll be thinking in terms of car miles or airplane miles. Well, what you learn on the Trail is foot miles—and believe me, that is a different concept altogether.

BELOW: Big Meadows, Shenandoah National Park, Virginia.

THE APPALACHIAN TRAIL

Walking slows you down. It makes you take the world in at a much more sedate and contemplative speed. Everything is up close and immediate and full of interest, and every distance is considerable. On foot a mile is a fair way, 10 miles is really far, 20 miles at the very limits of imagination. One of the great luxuries and astonishments of the Appalachian Trail is reaching a summit with a glorious top-of-the-world view and finding nothing but hills and unbroken forest rolling off to every horizon. There is nothing like it to make you realize how immense—not to mention incomparably lovely—this country of ours is.

But—and here's the perplexing corollary of that, which occurs to you almost simultaneously—it's not actually *that* big. What I mean by this is that from time to time you have to leave the Trail. You have to go into a town to resupply and do laundry, or the Trail takes you back to the built-up world, usually where it crosses an important river or traverses an open

BELOW: The Frye Brook Cataracts graced the early A.T. near Andover, Maine, but the footpath now lies about a mile and a half above them on the ridgeline.

valley between chains of hills, and abruptly you find yourself thrust back into a world of gas stations and shopping centers and fast-food places, and that is a disorienting shock indeed. Suddenly you realize that just as you are a small part of the forest, so the forest is a small part of a much busier landscape. The woods aren't so big after all. Out here in the commercial world, the woods—which an hour or two ago were so vast—are suddenly just a backdrop. The real business of the modern world, you realize, is business—shopping and consuming and making and spending, and driving between them all.

And that leads to the third discovery—the most obvious but also the most lasting—and that is what a wonderful thing are the eastern forests and how lucky we are to have them. It's a miracle really. Imagine if I said to you that I could put you in a time machine that would allow you to travel back 200 years or more to the world before the Industrial Revolution. Well, the Appalachian Trail is that time machine. It takes you to a landscape that would be wholly familiar to Daniel Boone and Davy Crockett and Lewis and Clark, a landscape of fresh air and tranquil greenery in the very heart of the most populous part of the country.

Of course, Boone and Crockett and Lewis and Clark would find a few differences these days. They would notice that several species of tree—hemlocks, dogwoods, red spruces, Fraser firs, hickories, mountain ashes, and the peerless sugar maples that give so much pleasure to millions of leaf-peepers every fall—are sometimes sick or dying in quite alarming numbers, and that others, like the graceful elms and mighty chestnuts, have vanished altogether. They would also notice that the woods are a good deal quieter than they once were, because the number of songbirds in the eastern United States has fallen by 50 percent. What they wouldn't know is that nearly all of this has happened in the last 50 years or so—which isn't a terribly long span.

That's why the most heartening initiative I have heard about in a long time is the ambitious, monumentally heroic, not-a-moment-too-soon endeavor known as the A.T. Megatransect, a collection of environmental-monitoring projects. That is, simply, a concerted effort by a variety of experts, institutions, and other willing partners to assess the full scale of threats to America's eastern woods and to plan programs of action to make sure they are as vibrant and lush and spiritually uplifting for future generations as they are for us today.

Because the Appalachian Trail travels through such timeless landscapes, it is easy to think of it as somehow permanent and self-sustaining. In fact, we can't be reminded too often that it exists only because decades ago some enlightened individuals had the vision and energy to get it built and because tens of thousands of volunteers have been heroically maintaining it ever since. We have a sacred duty—that is not putting it too strongly—to see that it remains healthy and vibrant for all time. We could, after all, be the last generation that gets the chance.

Which brings me to the final and most important thing I gained from hiking the Appalachian Trail—a combination of all the others—and that is namely a profound and lasting appreciation for the natural beauty of the country I grew up in. It isn't the America I remember from my childhood. It's an even better one.

OPPOSITE: A view from Mount Washington into the Great Gulf Wilderness in New Hampshire, also part of the White Mountain National Forest.

CHAPTER 1

Fashioning the Dream

The route of today's Appalachian Trail once delineated the colonial American frontier, sparsely settled by trappers and surveyors and small farmers in communities—more often than not—in the North and on scattered, more isolated plots in the South. In time, it was farmed out, mined, logged, and crossed by turnpikes directed toward a better life in the West.

As the government began to reclaim this mostly damaged land for broader public purposes early in the last century, a few Americans outside the mainstream began to see it as a place for a dream apart.

"The Appalachian Trail . . . one of the most extraordinary paths in the world, a footpath . . . did not come from use, from commerce, from necessity; it was deliberately planned and made, so that those who love the mountains could traverse them, so that our eastern wilderness would not become again a thing of the past," wrote one of the pillars of the Appalachian Trail project, Dr. Jean Stephenson, in 1941.

It is "a gift of nature which Americans gave to themselves," said Nash Castro at ceremonies marking the fiftieth anniversary of the footpath's completion. (Castro was then a New York State parks official who had played a pivotal role for the Trail as a young man in the Johnson White House.)

Today, it is known mostly for those who hike its whole length, but the path would not exist for those hikers had not another set of people across four generations conceived it, plotted it, maintained it, and protected it. They also added just enough land to its shoulders to make it seem like a separate place, for a life apart from "real life."

"Although new as an 'endless footpath through the wilderness,' the Trail itself seems age-old, so naturally does it fit into its surroundings. Just a path, now down a rough shoulder slope, now through old clearings sweet-scented with grasses in the sun, through dim forests, then up through scrub and out over bare mountain ledges, it seems it's been since the beginning; it seems it will be till the end," Dr. Stephenson wrote more than 70 years ago. At that time, much of the path was still on roads.

As she would insist if she were alive today, it is not a path *within* a place; rather it is a path *of* an arguably wilderness place. Its story developed disconnected from what we would generally see as the mainstream history of the last century. It is as if small knots of people responded to the original proposal for "a new approach to the problem of living" by evolving a place for parallel lives where living was not a problem.

It would be decades before the Trail came in from beyond the margins of America's story, became so much a part of the public estate and national landscape that it became a metaphor for challenge, a challenge Everyman could pursue.

A NEW APPROACH TO THE PROBLEM OF LIVING

It's 1925. Birth year of Paul Newman, Bobby Kennedy, Margaret Thatcher, Pol Pot, and B.B. King. And television. The Oscars ceremony hasn't been created yet, but Charlie Chaplin is working on *The Gold Rush*. In Germany, just out of prison, Adolf Hitler is completing *Mein Kampf* and reorganizing the Nazi party. Joseph Stalin is neutralizing Leon Trotsky. Ho Chi Minh is forming the Vietnamese Nationalist Party. Pablo Picasso is working on his trend-breaking *La danse* in Paris, Theodore Dreiser is wrapping up *An American Tragedy*, and H. L. Mencken is raving on in Baltimore, Maryland.

It's March, midway between the initial issues of *Time* and *The New Yorker* and the publication of *The Great Gatsby*, a wake-up call for the Jazz Age. Al Capone takes over the Chicago mob this month, the worst tornado in American history kills 700 in the Midwest, and Tennessee bans the teaching of evolutionary theory, setting the stage for John Scopes's arrest in May and trial in July, one of the first major news events covered by radio.

During the first week of March in Washington, D.C., most of the official side of the town, which was much smaller then, was absorbed with celebrations and preparations for the inauguration of Calvin Coolidge, who had just won against two major challengers, keeping on banking tycoon Andrew W. Mellon as treasury secretary and Herbert C. Hoover as commerce secretary. More quietly perhaps, J. Edgar Hoover was shaking up the Federal Bureau of Investigation, which he had been named to direct a few months before, and trying to deal with the resurgent Ku Klux Klan, which was reaching its zenith of strength after a long dormancy.

It was that Monday that, out of 212 invitees, less than two dozen people—mostly men, mostly from points north—sat down at 2:15 p.m. in a meeting room off the lobby of the then-grand and now-demolished Raleigh Hotel.

According to the meeting minutes, "the first Appalachian Trail conference was called . . . for the purpose of organizing a body of workers (representative of outdoor living and of the regions adjacent to the Appalachian range) to complete the building of the Appalachian Trail. This purpose was accomplished." The minutes apparently were written by Benton MacKaye (pronounced "Ma-Kye," rhyming with "sky").

The Regional Planning Association of America—MacKaye's workplace then, to the extent he had one—had asked the Federated Societies on Planning and Parks to call the meeting. The Federated Societies was a coalition of the American Civic Association, the American Institute of Park Executives and American Park Society, and the National Conference on State Parks. Its president, Frederic A. Delano, described it as "a pooling of common interests and not a compromise of conflicting interests," an explanation later used to define the relationship between the Appalachian Trail Conference (ATC) and autonomous clubs and their volunteers who undertook the bulk of the work of maintaining the Trail and such facilities as shelters, privies, and bridges.

MacKaye had spent the better part of the previous four years proselytizing from Boston, Massachusetts, to Washington on behalf of the Appalachian Trail project he had proposed in October 1921 in an article in the *Journal of the American Institute of Architects*. The journal's editor and another promoter of the concept, Clarence S. Stein, was secretary of the Regional Planning Association, which was based in New York City.

The article, "An Appalachian Trail: A Project in Regional Planning," was in many ways a classical treatise—half-pragmatic, half-philosophical—fully in keeping with the utopian intellectual climate of the urban East following World War I. Its tenets were, in part, a reaction to the shock of the war, to the Bolshevik Revolution in imperial Russia, and to the emerging petroleum technology (and ultimately petrochemical and pharmaceutical technology) on top of nearly a century of rapid industrialization fueled by coal and wood and steam.

A close reading of the article confirms that he was proposing an ambitious social and political agenda for an America on the postwar move. A hiking trail was only part of the plan. Ironically, while he proposed an agenda for the mainstream, the project's acolytes would seize upon the Trail as a way to step aside from it.

MacKaye plainly didn't like where America was moving, especially by motor vehicle and especially into ever more crowded cities. He presented the Trail concept as "a new approach to the problem of living"—a means both "to reduce the day's drudgery" and to improve the quality of American leisure, the quantity of which had been increased by labor-saving devices, by the automobiles 15 percent of the population now owned, and by the slow acceptance of the radical eight-hour workday.

The article proposed an extended wilderness along the Appalachian crests as a crucial line of defense against both demoralization of urban laborers (by providing a refuge for contemplation in a natural setting) and "the lure of militarism" (by channeling primal heroic instincts into care

Proposed
APPALACHIAN TRAIL
(A Crestline Footpath)

Main Trail
Branch or Extension
Motor Road Connection

Pivotal Sections

① Berkshire — New England
② Palisades Park — N.Y.-N.J.
③ᴀ Lehigh ⎱ Pennsylvania
③ʙ Susquehanna ⎰
④ Shenandoah — Cent. Appal'ns
⑤ᴀ Gt. Smokies ⎱ So. Appal'ns
⑤ʙ Blue Ridge ⎰

of the countryside). MacKaye also thought it would be helpful in fighting forest fires and would provide 40,000 jobs for its construction: the practical aspect many socioeconomic thinkers of the day were careful to include in their more politically radical proposals.

But, to say that MacKaye's article began the project is to overlook the aspirations of a strong pre-1921 hiking or "tramping" movement in New England and a newly emerging one in New York. Seeing the article as the start of the project also would presume that the A.T. concept emerged overnight, without the influence of other personalities and experiences on MacKaye, a lean, wiry, highly active, 42-year-old Yankee's Yankee—not unlike the man in the White House, but considerably more voluble and rustic. Those influences included not only his intellectual associates and his family, but also several key leaders of established hiking organizations who were friends from his college days.

INITIAL TRAIL-BUILDING EFFORTS

The first two decades of the 20th century saw a broad array of path-building efforts by small clubs in New England and New York's Hudson River Valley. Many who spearheaded those efforts dreamed of a "grand trunk" trail, stretching the entire length of the eastern Appalachian ridge lands.

The Long Trail's James P. Taylor in Vermont; columnist Allen Chamberlain of the *Boston Evening Transcript*, a hiker and past president of the Appalachian Mountain Club (AMC), which was founded in 1876 to build White Mountains trails; New Hampshire forester Philip W. Ayres; and all of their organizations initiated a meeting late in 1916 to form the New England Trail Conference (NETC). Its purpose was to coordinate the work of that region's trail-making agencies and clubs.

Taylor had been partly responsible for bringing Ayres into the fold. Representing the Society for the Protection of New Hampshire Forests, Ayres was seeking ways to build a pro-forests coalition and found one in the hiking and trail-building community. In 1914, he was a major force behind the establishment of the White Mountain National Forest (WMNF)—the first national forest in the East. Longer trails and unified systems of trails—both within regions and between regions—were reoccurring topics among those men and their organizations at meetings throughout the prewar years.

Laura and the late Guy Waterman, ATC members who published a history of northeastern trail-building in the 1980s, attribute the feverish activity of this period in New England, New York, and New Jersey to the emergence of the automobile. It changed the pattern of trail-building. Loops and mountain climbs centered on a particular mountain vacation spot gave way to a preference for through-trails connecting mountain ranges, simply because hikers could more easily travel to other, less-developed trailheads.

The rise of the affordable automobile created circular tensions that would underlie at least the first four decades of Appalachian Trail history: MacKaye's proposal was in part an attack on the metropolis-clogging and wilderness-defiling automobiles that, ironically, allowed trail-builders to blaze longer footpaths, allowed hikers the time and means to travel farther to trek, and, still within MacKaye's lifetime, ultimately threatened the continuity of those long-distance trails.

OPPOSITE AND ABOVE: Myron Avery's infamous wheel is the centerpiece of a collection of early Potomac Appalachian Trail Club tools for clearing and measuring the footpath in the 1920s and 1930s.

BENTON MACKAYE'S VISION

All that dreaming and what-if activity among New England club leaders was one impetus toward "the big one" in eastern trail-building circles, the culmination of many years of trail-builders' hopes and plans. The other was, of course, MacKaye, since it was his full-length proposal that came to fruition. As in the case of any celebrated dreamer, philosopher, or grand visionary, MacKaye's personal background necessarily became an integral part of the foundation of his proposals.

In a 1964 message to the sixteenth Appalachian Trail conference, MacKaye said his "dream . . . may well have originated" at the end of a hike to the peak of Vermont's Stratton

Mountain in July 1900. Climbing to the top of a tree for better views, he wrote, "I felt as if atop the world, with a sort of 'planetary feeling' . . . . Would a footpath someday reach [far-southern peaks] from where I was then perched?"

In his later years, MacKaye was far from consistent in his recollections of the source of the A.T. idea. Biographer Larry Anderson notes that most versions indicate the idea did evolve to a marked extent from his turn-of-the-century hikes and backcountry explorations. MacKaye's diaries from the 1920s also clearly show friendships with key individuals in New England hiking clubs and a distinct pattern of what, in today's jargon, would be called "networking" with them, both before and after his 1921 article.

During this period, MacKaye noted, he also became acquainted with the AMC's Allen Chamberlain, the Boston columnist. "It was during these experiences (summers between 1897 and 1912) that my own notions of a north-south mountain footway must have been conceived," MacKaye wrote.

It would be a mistake to assume that in the *Journal* article MacKaye was advocating a *hiking* utopia—although he did cast his idea in terms of a footpath, and he did relish the outdoors and relatively short hikes and backpacking trips. That said, hiking for its own sake, as recreation or a means to personal fulfillment, was not the goal he espoused.

MacKaye's work after college documents a man seeking to offset what he saw as the negative effects on mankind of rapid mechanization and urbanization. He sought regeneration of the human spirit through what he termed "harmony with primeval influences." To him, walking was a means to the intermediate end of understanding the forest civilization, which in turn was the means to the ultimate end of understanding human civilization.

In a February 1935 letter, MacKaye said that his brother's "last written words to me were about the creative value of the wilderness. From him I drew my fundamental inspiration; and, in a sense (though he did not conceive the scheme itself), he was the real father of the Appalachian Trail."

MacKaye, born in 1879 in Stamford, Connecticut, was the sixth child and last son of a then-famous playwright, actor, and inventor, James Steele MacKaye, and the former Mary Ellen (Mollie) Keith Medberry. His extended family was large and dominated by artistic siblings, including another successful playwright and a novelist, although it also included patent attorneys and newspaper reporters.

From the time he was nine, MacKaye began living year-round at the family retreat in rural Shirley Center, Massachusetts, northwest of Boston and about 10 miles from the New Hampshire line. The retreat was two rundown houses on a few acres, according to biographer Larry Anderson. MacKaye apparently spent much of his time wandering the countryside around that small village, alone or under the guidance of a neighboring farmer.

At age 14, he began an intensive, documented countryside exploration, compiling a journal of nine "expeditions"—combining walking with investigation of the natural environment—on which his 1969 book, *Expedition Nine*, was based. Four years later, in 1897, he had that first taste of "wilderness" he would recall as the genesis of his A.T. notions: bicycling from Boston with college

OPPOSITE: Benton MacKaye often said he got the inspiration for the A.T. while sitting in a tree on Stratton Mountain in southern Vermont.

friends to Tremont Mountain in New Hampshire and then hiking into the backcountry. He saw it then as "a second world—and promise!"

After several financially strapped years and after graduating in forestry from Harvard College in 1905, he joined the new U.S. Forest Service under Gifford Pinchot. MacKaye later recalled a meeting of the Society of American Foresters at Pinchot's home in "about 1912" to which he read a new paper by his friend, Allen Chamberlain. "[It] was, I think, the first dissertation on long-distance footways," he wrote. Pinchot would later endorse MacKaye's vision for "an Appalachian Trail for recreation, for health and recuperation, and for employment on the land."

By his early thirties, MacKaye's focus shifted from science, woodlot management, and other aspects of silviculture to the humanities: the effect of resource management on humans, from lumberjacks and landowners to forest visitors. "Regional planning" as an occupational discipline seemed to capture his interests, although he and his close-knit Washington friends were most active in opposing the brewing war in Europe.

In 1918, Assistant Labor Secretary Louis F. Post, owner of a political journal, had MacKaye transferred to the Department of Labor (itself only five years old as a separate department), where he and Secretary William B. Wilson were developing policies intended to create jobs through better use of natural resources. All three felt that the country's natural resources had been abused by the speculation that accompanied the land-grant and homesteading statutes (which dated back through Abraham Lincoln to Thomas Jefferson) and by the pace of America's post-Civil War industrial revolution.

In a major 1919 report, keyed to the labor surplus created by post-World War I demobilization, MacKaye proposed a new program of federal land colonization: the government would establish farm, forest, and mining communities organized around economic cooperation, on publicly owned land. The agricultural part of the plan went so far as to have the government preplowing fields and providing barns, stock, and machinery, so settling farmers would not be crippled by start-up costs.

Legislation embodying the report's proposals was killed by hostile congressional committees in an increasingly conservative Washington, by the Agriculture and Interior departments' opposition, by farm organizations' attacks, and by the prevailing view, even then, that fewer, more intensive farmers and steadier industrial employment were the solutions to economic stagnation. Funds for MacKaye's work were cut off, and he was out of the department by July 1919.

In 1920, MacKaye began a lifelong association with Charles Harris Whitaker, editor of the *Journal of the American Institute of Architects*, and part of the Washington circle that was infatuated with socialist events in Russia. Whitaker was an ardent proponent of the "garden cities" or "new towns" in vogue in English planning circles that would not become as popular in the United States until the 1960s and 1970s. They worked together on a regional plan for seven Northern Tier states that involved "new towns" clustered near raw materials and power sources connected to consuming towns by postal roads: calculated use of resources, with a social and economic conscience.

In mid-1920, MacKaye took a job as an editorial writer at a Milwaukee newspaper. However, his wife—leading suffrage activist Jesse Belle Hardy Stubbs, who went by "Betty" and whom he had

ABOVE: Clarence Stein (left) and Benton MacKaye (right) in the Cosmos Club garden in Washington, D.C., in June 1964. OPPOSITE: Reclaimed pasture in southwest Virginia.

married in 1915—became increasingly mentally frail. She stirred up a local furor that led to MacKaye's quitting the newspaper and heading by year's end to New York. On April 18, 1921, Betty MacKaye jumped to her death in New York's East River. She had run to the bridge from Grand Central Station, where they were buying train tickets to the country so she, often depressed, could rest.

Not having any children of his own but accustomed from his Washington years to living within a circle of intellectual activists, MacKaye constructed for the rest of his years a new, alternative family of planning associates, the men and women who would promote the early Trail, and such successful writers as urban-life theorist Lewis Mumford. The "family" would come to include Tennessee attorney Harvey Broome and the other conservationists with whom he would found the Wilderness Society in the 1930s, after a continuous Appalachian Trail became a reality as a hiking footpath and he had a falling-out with the people who actually had made it real.

But, more immediately, MacKaye was only slowly regaining his balance following his wife's suicide. Charles Whitaker urged him to come to his northwestern New Jersey farm and stay until he worked his way through his grief. MacKaye accepted and, once there, started working out "recreation project" and "Appal. Trail" ideas on paper. After reading MacKaye's notes, Whitaker invited Clarence Stein, chairman of the committee on community planning of the Washington-based American Institute of Architects (AIA), to meet them at Hudson Guild Farm at Netcong in the New Jersey

OUTINGS---A GREAT TRAIL FROM MAINE TO GEORGIA

2,000-Mile Trail On Appalachian Ridges Planned

Benton MacKaye's Idea Supported by Institute Of Architects

New York and New Jersey Hikers Asked to Carry Path Through Their Section

By Raymond H. Torrey

Some mighty big things are coming out of this trail movement in the next few years if its development grows at the pace it now shows. The spread of idea of promoting wholesome outdoor recreation through trails for hikers and mountain climbers has been encouraged by many factors in the last two or three years, and some new urge is constantly appearing.

For a long time after its formation, in 1876, the Appalachian Mountain Club was about the only trail-making organization in the United States. It worked steadily for thirty years, but in the last ten its activities have been especially wide and fruitful in making trails in the White Mountains and in other parts of New Hampshire and in adjoining Maine. A dozen years ago the Green Mountain Club began work in Vermont and has made the famous Long Trail. A score of local trail-making clubs have also done excellent work in New England. Meanwhile, hiking clubs and recreation trail-making forces have spread across the country to the Pacific, where they have developed great vigor.

In New York State such trails as existed for for hikers "just grew" and were scattered and local. It was not until the last five years or so that organized work on systematic lines was attempted. The Conservation Commission began a trail system in the Adirondacks, which will be continued by the new Adirondack Mountain Club, which promises to be a useful and important force for outdoor recreation. Two years ago delegates from the principal New York City walking clubs, the New York sections of the Appalachian and Green Mountain Clubs, the Fresh Air and Tramp and Trail Clubs, and some individuals formed the Palisades Interstate Park Trail Conference, which, with the sanction of the manager of that park, Major W. A. Welch, made a twenty-five-mile trail from Tuxedo to Jones Point, on the Hudson. The same workers have extended this path northward along the west side of the Hudson, over Bear Mountain. The New Jersey State Forestry Department has made about eight miles of trail in the Stokes Reservation on the summit of Kittatinny Mountain, north-east from Culver Gap. These two paths were the only trails of consid-

Appalachian Trail *suggested by* Benton MacKaye, *for the committee on community planning of the American Inst. of Architects*

INSET AT RIGHT SHOWS New York and New Jersey SECTION of PROJECTED TRAIL...

Major Welch, approved this idea. The R-D Trail would naturally fall into the system; so would the Kittatinny forestry trail. The rest of Mr. MacKaye's route through the two States follows lines suggested by considerations of scenic beauty and of directness; along the northern ridge of the Highlands east of the Hudson to Breakneck Ridge, crossing the river either by the Newburgh-Beacon ferry or by the proposed bridge at Anthony's Nose; on the R-D Trail to Tuxedo west by wood roads to Greenwood Lake, and over Wawayanda Mountain to the valley of the Wallkill, on to the Kittatinny Range, taking up the forestry trail, and along this ridge to Water Gap.

Mr. MacKaye and Mr. Stein propose to leave the carrying out of the work in this section entirely to such an organization of hiking club delegates as may be formed, since they include many outdoor folks experienced in such work in New England. The work for the present would consist of scouting for the best and most feasible routes, as many problems as to crossing some areas would have to be solved.

Over the Delaware is somewhat unknown country, so far as the existence of trail building organizations or material for them is concerned. Mr. MacKaye thinks that nuclei for trail making clubs might be found in some college communities, such as Lafayette College at Easton, Pa., and the University of Virginia at Charlottesville, and in centres like Harrisburg, Pa.,

"The long brown path before me, leading wherever I choose."
— *Walt Whitman.*

Major W. A. Welch, general manager of the Palisades Interstate Park, has already built a log bridge across Popolopen Creek, at the point where the new extension of the Ramapo-Dunderberg Trail from the Timp Pass over West and Bear Mountains crosses this swift and rocky stream. He acted promptly on the suggestion of trail makers, who located the crossing only a few weeks ago. Major Welch has also prepared quantity of markers for the extension, which will be known as the "Timp-Torne" trail, from its present northern terminus on Popolopen Torne. The markers will be similar in shape to the R-D signs, with the initials "T-T" for "Timp-Torne" and a red square. This will be a highly scenic trail and can easily be done in a day's tramp.

Major Welch writes to the editor of the Outing Page that he has obtained consents from the Witherbee-Sherman Real Estate Corporation, which owns the property between the top of Long Mountain and the Popolopen Creek Valley, for the continuation

Queensboro Bridge to Jamaica and Mineola and return.

The New York State Conservation Commission announces an opportunity to any one who wishes to plant black walnut trees. It has been advised by J. W. Calland, forester of the Miami Conservancy District, that owing to a change in plans for flood prevention work in that section of Ohio he has 100,000 one-year-old black walnut trees which may be had at practically the cost of digging, packing, boxing, and hauling, $1.20 per hundred in lots of 500 to 2,500, or $1 per hundred in lots of more than 2,500.

The Tramp and Trail Club will picnic on the Palisades to-morrow afternoon, under leadership of E. Cecil Earle. On Sunday the club will hike in the hills north of Paterson, N. J., starting at Goffle Brook, Hawthorne, going over the Goffle Ridge, to the county line, then west to High Mountain and south along the Preakness Range to Haledon, under the leadership of Miss Mabel A. Godfrey.

The Fresh Air Club will do the

Scouts Working on White Bar Trail

40-Mile Route Circles Lake Kanawauke Camps

Path With Permanent Camps in Wildest Sections of Interstate Park

When plans now being carried out are accomplished, a Scout will be able to go on a week's hike in the region of the Lake Kanawauke headquarters in the Interstate Park without carrying grub or shelter tents. This is the plan of Chief Gordon of this Scout centre and it is now being carried out by Scouts of Troop 208, The Bronx.

A trail is being laid out to encircle the Lake Kanawauke camps. Its total length will be over 40 level miles as measured on a map. The hills and valleys will make this distance 25 to 50 per cent more. It will be called the White Bar Trail. It is not a brand new trail, such as the Ramapo-Dunderberg system, but is a linking of old wood trails already in existence. Where there were none suitable, a new trail will be cut. It was started several years ago and the various portions marked. Unfortunately, the markers used—sticks about a foot long, painted white—were too tempting to some boys, who took them as souvenirs, or perhaps used them as kindling for a fire. The result was that the trail was often without marks at all, and it was easy to get lost, especially in the wild section around Breakneck Mountain.

To remedy this defect metal signs, painted and stenciled, are now in the course of preparation. Some of these have already been put up and mark the first part of the trail. They are firmly fastened to the trees at a distance from the ground which makes them easy to see but still keeps them from souvenir hunters. Of nearly a hundred wooden markers put up on one section last July only three were found in place by a party which went through on Lincoln's Birthday.

To cover the whole trail will require a hike of five and a half days. In providing for accommodations at night it is Chief Gordon's plan to establish a series of five camps at one-day (about ten-mile) intervals on the way. They will be tents this summer, but it is hoped that park lean-tos will eventually be built. A man will be stationed at each of these camps who will be responsible for the comfort of hiking parties as they come in at night. A hot meal will be ready for them and shelter tents will be ready to pitch. In the morning they will have breakfast and be given grub for their

Many Canoeing Strea

By John Whitm

Geogra...nditions, within a 100-mi...such that canoeists of the metropoli-

Highlands. Stein, also a garden-city advocate, had designed some of the buildings at the farm, an environmental-education retreat and summer working-vacation spot for boys. The farm was maintained by the Hudson Guild Settlement House, a volunteer-based social-services offspring of Britain's Ethical Culture movement; it still serves Manhattan's working-class Chelsea neighborhoods.

On Sunday, July 10, 1921, the three men met at the farm, with Whitaker agreeing to publish MacKaye's article and Stein agreeing to promote the ideas through his contacts. The farm would become MacKaye's workplace for months at a time over the ensuing three or four years. "The meeting also initiated a close friendship between MacKaye and Stein that lasted until the year they both died, in 1975," biographer Larry Anderson wrote. "Stein would become MacKaye's most significant professional and financial patron."

"On that July Sunday half a century ago, the seed of our Trail was planted. Except for the two men named, it would never have come to pass," MacKaye wrote to ATC Chairman Stanley A. Murray nearly 50 years later.

THE 1921 CONCEPT

The 1921 concept was aimed at urban workers who, MacKaye hoped, would return from an Appalachian-crest sojourn determined to use industrialism "as a means in life and not as an end in itself." He included many of the elements of his 1919 Labor Department report: a footpath as a baseline for self-sufficient, separated camps and communities developed to meet economic and social needs; the rational use of natural resources and the psychological after-effects of their environment for a more livable world; conscious planning for leisure as well as jobs; and designing for living rather than solely for profit.

Each element of the proposal was intended to appeal to a particular interest group, from hikers to labor unions. Despite his ties to Stein, Mumford, and the others behind the 1925 meeting, MacKaye would abandon virtually all the community-planning aspects as he organized support for the Trail concept and found that the recreational and escaping-the-city psychological values had popular appeal while the other elements did not.

Why did MacKaye's proposal take off when other northeasterners' dreams did not? At least for the period of the early to mid-1920s, a three-part answer can be suggested.

First, MacKaye's was a grander—and thus more inspiring—vision uncomplicated by practical, field-level details, and, until later, "action plans."

Second, his article was replete with hints about the publicity value of one aspect of the proposal or another, which he intended to exploit and was encouraging supporters to exploit as well. The record is full of evidence that, with help from former mentors such as Louis Post, he courted reporters and columnists who would give the idea more exposure. Newspaper editors in all regions often appear on the participants' list from those early meetings. For example, in a 1969 letter to Stanley Murray, MacKaye paid homage to the New York–New Jersey area men with whom he worked most closely in the early 1920s, specifically Raymond H. Torrey, who edited the outdoors pages for the *New York Evening Post* and wrote a regular column, The Long Brown Path. Not unlike the AMC's Chamberlain, Torrey was a leader of the young New York–New Jersey Trail Conference, formed during a planning meeting with MacKaye and others to build trails in New Jersey and finish and maintain many trails in New York, including the new Appalachian Trail.

Third, he, Stein, and Whitaker worked their social and professional connections vigorously. A cover note by Stein on reprints of MacKaye's 1921 article was an eloquent call to action that would make any populist political candidate proud: Workers' homes are congested, in undesirable neighborhoods; parks are inadequate; cities are devouring farms and forests; "it is as though man had been created for industry and not industry to serve man's need."

Stein continued:

> We need the big sweep of hills or sea as tonic for our jaded nerves—And so Mr. Benton MacKaye offers us a new theme in regional planning. It is not a plan for more efficient use of labor, but a plan of escape. He would as far as practicable conserve the whole stretch of the Appalachian Mountains for recreation. Recreation in the biggest senses—the recreation of the spirit that is being crushed by the machinery of the modern industrial city—the spirit of fellowship and cooperation.

Stein also noted the foundations already laid for a north-south through-trail by AMC, the Green Mountain Club, and others in the New England Trail Conference; a new AMC chapter in Asheville (which broke away as the Carolina Mountain Club in June 1923); the success of the Palisades Interstate Parkway in New York and New Jersey; and more utopian cooperative farms and camps being developed in New Jersey and Pennsylvania. As an organizing vehicle, as well as a promotional force, Stein volunteered his AIA committee.

THE NEXT STEPS

Often on his own the next two years, MacKaye started in Boston to work on the NETC and AMC leaderships, moved on to New Hampshire and the forestry leadership there, and then to New York, where he collected support from the Boy Scouts and attended meeting upon meeting with Torrey. At one of the meetings, he connected with J. Ashton Allis, a banker who previously had proposed a trail from Delaware Water Gap to New England, and retired Army Major William A. Welch.

Welch, who also was on a commission seeking locations for two newly authorized southern national parks, had been general manager and chief engineer of the Palisades Interstate Park Commission since the turn of the century. He had called together Torrey and other hiking-organization representatives in 1920 to form a new organization to help him plan a network of trails that would make Bear Mountain–Harriman State Park on the Hudson River more accessible to the public. That organization soon became the New York–New Jersey Trail Conference. The next day, Torrey published a lengthy column with a near-banner headline—"A Great Trail from Maine to Georgia"—accompanied by a version of MacKaye's map of the route (see page 26).

MacKaye moved on to Washington, D.C., to economist L. F. Schmeckebier of the Brookings Institution and geologist Francois E. Matthes of the U.S. Geological Survey, both leaders of outdoors groups. With them in April 1922, he formed an "Appalachian Trail Committee of Washington." The group also included a Scripps-McCray newspaper reporter, two U.S. Forest Service officials, and Louis Post, his former mentor from the Labor Department. A handful of U.S. Department of Agriculture officials who attended this meeting later formed part of the core of the Potomac Appalachian Trail Club, which became the most dynamic of the initial trailblazers.

MacKaye spent that spring and summer drafting a constitution for what he then foresaw as "The Appalachian Trail, Inc.," and writing letters to officials and other interested men, especially Forest Service connections in the South. MacKaye, Stein, and others thought it would be hardest to stimulate interest in the Trail in the South because the region had fewer hiking organizations and constructed trails than New England and the New York metropolitan area.

"By sheer force of his idea and his personality, MacKaye began stitching together the network of enthusiasts and public officials who would eventually comprise a permanent community of trail-builders," Larry Anderson wrote of this missionary tour.

Among those he wrote or visited were Dr. Halstead S. Hedges of Charlottesville, Virginia, who made a number of scouting trips in the Shenandoah Valley; Pisgah National Forest Supervisor Verne Rhoades, who would set an example for other public lands by converting an existing footpath there into the A.T.; Clinton G. Smith, supervisor of Cherokee National

OPPOSITE: L. F. Schmeckebier, an early ATC trail maintainer, demonstrates proper blazing technique.
ABOVE: First view of Katahdin in the distance for northbound thru-hikers.

Forest, who did the same; and Paul M. Fink of Jonesborough, Tennessee, a banker friend of Massachusetts landscape architect Harlan P. Kelsey and acquaintance of National Park Service Director Arno Cammerer. Fink, one of the more colorful A.T. pioneers, would be the only one to outlive MacKaye.

Kelsey, also a nurseryman, served with Welch on the commission identifying lands for what would become the Shenandoah and Great Smoky Mountains national parks. MacKaye gave credit in 1969 to Kelsey as author of the phrase, "From Maine to Georgia," as the official motto for the Trail.

In November 1922, MacKaye, his brother James, and Stein regrouped at Shirley Center, Massachusetts, to review the year's work and lay out "steps to fill the gaps." In December, NETC Chairman Albert Turner "'batched it' with me on Christmas Day at my home in Shirley Center," MacKaye recalled. The next month brought them together again at the annual meeting of the NETC. Sturgis Pray, his camp teacher and hiking companion in 1897, spoke, as did MacKaye. NETC passed a resolution approving the A.T. concept. The following summer, MacKaye himself actually scouted and mapped potential Trail locations in northwestern New Jersey, a rare foray for him into the actual work of trailblazing.

Meanwhile, work on building a new trail specifically as a part of the Appalachian Trail was underway in the Hudson River Valley. Bear Mountain Bridge, a private project partly organized by Welch, was under construction at the time across the Hudson at Harriman State Park. That seemed the ideal spot to bring the Trail from New England across the river and toward the Delaware Water Gap at the Pennsylvania line. So, the New York–New Jersey Trail Conference and

ABOVE AND OPPOSITE: From the original copper square designed by Major Welch and made by New York State parks crews, the traditional and now-trademarked A.T. symbol evolved through several iterations before the white blaze superseded it.

the indefatigable Raymond Torrey had gone to work. The first section, from the Bear Mountain Bridge to the Ramapo River south of Arden, was completed in 1923.

In late October of that year, the pioneers gathered at the Bear Mountain Inn, just downriver from the bridge and only a few dozen steps from the new A.T. section, which officially opened on October 7. That three-day meeting "did for the Hudson–Delaware section what the January NETC meeting did for the New England section"—clinching work already done and crystallizing plans for the next steps, according to MacKaye.

On its last day, the conferees agreed to adopt as a Trail marker a monogram designed by Welch, with the crossbar of the 'A' serving as the top of the 'T.' This emblem was embossed on a square piece of copper with "Appalachian Trail–Palisades Interstate Park Section" in raised relief.

THE REGIONAL PLANNING ASSOCIATION

The Regional Planning Association, which first met in 1923, included MacKaye, Stein, Mumford, and Whitaker among its 11 charter members. All were critics of the haphazard growth of U.S. cities, advocates of deliberate planning of growth and resource use, and believers in the proposed A.T. as a model of regional planning that might spark popular support for their positions.

Toward the end of 1924, the Regional Planning Association (RPA) sponsors of the A.T. idea decided it was time to pass the project on to a more focused central organization, homing in at a December meeting of the general council of the National Conference on Outdoor Recreation in

Washington, D.C. The participants were told by Commerce Secretary Herbert Hoover that their objective was "to make life less drab." The RPA soon requested the Federated Societies to convene an "Appalachian Trail conference" in Washington. Harlean James, the federation's executive secretary who would become the ATC's volunteer secretary for its first 16 years, did so.

Members of the RPA met two or three times a week, with occasional weekend retreats at Hudson Guild Farm that included square dancing and folk singing led by MacKaye. (RPA's active years ended with Franklin D. Roosevelt's election as president in 1932 and the creation of the Tennessee Valley Authority, for which MacKaye would eventually work and which Mumford considered "the ripest fruit of two generations of regional thinking.")

THE HISTORIC 1925 MEETING

The conferees spent the first afternoon of March 2, 1925, talking about the potential of the A.T. project, with MacKaye leading off:

> Its ultimate purpose is to conserve, use, and enjoy the mountain hinterland . . . . The Trail (or system of trails) is a means for making the land accessible. The Appalachian Trail is to this Appalachian region what the Pacific Railway was to the Far West—a means of "opening up" the country. But a very different kind of "opening up." Instead of a railway we want a "trailway" . . .
>
> Like the railway, the trailway should be a functioning service. It embodies three main necessities: (1) shelter and food (a series of camps and stores); (2) conveyance to and from the neighboring cities, by rail and motor; (3) the footpath or trail itself connecting the camps.
>
> But, unlike the railway, the trailway must preserve (and develop) a certain environment. Otherwise, its whole point is lost. The railway "opens up" a country as a site for civilization; the trailway should "open up" a country as an escape from civilization . . . . The path of the trailway should be as "pathless" as possible; it should be the minimum consistent with practical accessibility.
>
> But, railway and trailway, each one is *a way*—each "goes somewhere." Each has the lure of discovery—of a country's penetration and unfolding. The hinterland we would unfold is not that from Cape to Cairo, but that from Maine to Georgia.

The group agreed to his suggestion that the trail-building effort be divided into five regions, with one or two particular sections to focus on within each. He thought it could all be done within 15 months, in time for the United States' 150th anniversary. In reality, it required another 12 years.

Others spoke of the potential of specific aspects—many of which would resonate today. F. E. Matthes of the U.S. Geological Survey foresaw both nature-guide and historic-guide services. For him, the minutes recalled, the ultimate purpose of the A.T. was "to develop an environment wherein the people themselves (and not merely their experts) may experience—through contact

and not mere print—a basic comprehension of the forces of nature (evident in forest growth, in water power, and otherwise) and of the conservation, use, and enjoyment thereof." Fred F. Schuetz of the Scout Leaders Association, who would spend the rest of his life involved with the ATC, extolled "tributary trails" from cities to the ridgecrests. Arthur Comey, secretary of the New England Trail Conference, gave a workshop a half century before its time on "going light," so that "the knapsack should serve as an instrument and not an impediment in the art of outdoor living."

With the Trail route more advanced in New England, New York, and New Jersey, the meeting the next morning concentrated on other regions. Clinton Smith of the U.S. Forest Service showed the possibilities allowed by that agency's trails system in the central and southern Appalachian national forests, while others addressed the challenges of a trail in the two proposed national parks and the possibilities between Pennsylvania and Maryland.

The Trail's "main line" under the plans adopted at that meeting would run an estimated 1,700 miles from Mount Washington in New Hampshire to Cohutta Mountain in Georgia. Extensions were proposed to Katahdin in Maine, to Lookout Mountain in Tennessee, and then to Birmingham, Alabama. "Branch lines" were projected on the Long Trail in Vermont; from New Jersey into the Catskills; from Harpers Ferry, West Virginia, up toward Buffalo, New York; from the Tennessee River into Kentucky; and from Grandfather Mountain in North Carolina toward Atlanta, Georgia.

After a luncheon speech by Stephen Mather, first director of the National Park Service and an advocate of trails in parks, William Welch called the business part of the meeting to order. The

OPPOSITE: The (replaced) Indian Gap Shelter in Great Smoky Mountains National Park was typical of hiker lean-tos built in the 1930s by the CCC and other government crews.
ABOVE: The rare view of Harpers Ferry, West Virginia, from the Virginia side of the Potomac River, shows the bridges (left) taking the original A.T. into town and its immediate exit (right) into Maryland, before 1936 floods took them all out.

Conference was made a permanent body (although it would be almost 12 years before it would be incorporated as such) and a provisional constitution was adopted. That constitution, written by MacKaye, provided for management of ATC affairs by a 15-member executive committee—two members from each region and five chosen at large.

Welch was elected chairman, Torrey treasurer, James secretary, and MacKaye field organizer. That office, briefly held, would be MacKaye's only official position within the Appalachian Trail project, now firmly a recreational project rather than a utopian social project.

The composition of that initial executive committee underscores a key tradition of the Trail project: what some have viewed as an experiment in participatory democracy, what others call cooperative management of national resources, and what still others describe as a unique partnership between the public and private sectors.

As MacKaye biographer Larry Anderson put it, "The principle of local groups, federated under the gentle guidance of a modest central organization, working and playing on the terrain they knew and loved, would provide the key to the project's eventual completion and success." Moreover, although trail-building for hiking became the overwhelming focus of the project for decades to come, many of the sentiments of pioneers such as MacKaye, Stein, and Matthes would be revived to inform the organization's thrusts in the 21st century.

In addition to the five regional divisions of the Conference, seats on the committee were specifically allocated to Colonel W.B. Greeley, chief of the U.S. Forest Service, and Pisgah National Forest Supervisor Verne Rhoades, who was named vice chairman. Other seats were allotted to the Regional Planning Association (Stein), the Federated Societies (Welch), and the National Conference on Outdoor Recreation (Chauncey J. Hamlin). Arthur Comey and Charles P. Cooper of Rutland, Vermont, held NETC seats. Torrey and Frank Place represented the New York–New Jersey Trail Conference. A.E. Rupp, chief of the state department of lands and waters, and J. Bruce Byall represented the Pennsylvania region. Dr. Halstead S. Hedges of the University of Virginia and G. Freeman Pollock, president of the Northern Virginia Park Association, represented their state. Rhoades and Paul Fink covered the rest of the South.

G. ARTHUR PERKINS

Despite the major step forward in coordination of the project and organization of additional trail-builders, actual work in terms of completed Trail mileage fell off. Planning and publicity went on, carefully and in detail, but field progress—in recruitment of volunteers and construction of the Trail—lost momentum due to lack of field leadership.

Then, in 1926, a retired Hartford, Connecticut, police-court judge, G. Arthur Perkins, appointed to fill a vacancy from New England on the executive committee, breathed new life into the project. After a summer spent in New Hampshire's White Mountains in the early 1920s, the Yale-educated "J.P." (short for Judge Perkins), joined the Appalachian Mountain Club for its excursions program. He quickly became hooked on exploring Katahdin. In addition to Connecticut trail work, he went on to galvanize Massachusetts and Pennsylvania supporters and, perhaps most importantly, connect with a 27-year-old Harvard Law School graduate and admiralty lawyer—Myron H. Avery.

At the annual January meeting of NETC in Boston in 1927, MacKaye delivered a speech entitled "Outdoor Culture: The Philosophy of Through Trails." Borrowing themes developed by ATC Executive Committee member Chauncey Hamlin, it comes across on paper today as a true tub-thumping political oration on behalf of the A.T. project.

He talked of man's utopias as pipe dreams, citing real heroes that made major discoveries and Douglas Fairbanks's film heroes, mere vicarious escapes from the humdrum. He saw the A.T. as a means for every man to become a Magellan. Harmony between man and nature lies in regional planning, he asserted. American cities represent humans' tendency to "over-civilize;" they are as "spreading, unthinking, ruthless" as a glacier. MacKaye said he hoped for development of a modern American Barbarian, "a rough and ready engineer" and explorer who would mount the crests of the Appalachians "and open war on the further encroachment of his mechanized Utopia . . . . [The] philosophy of through trails . . . is to organize a Barbarian invasion . . . . The Appalachian Range should be placed in public hands and become the site for a Barbarian Utopia," he declared, more than four decades before the Congress would agree. "This philosophy . . . is 'the why' of the Appalachian Trail, which—let us hope—may some day form the base for the strategy of a 'Barbarian invasion,' and for the development of a Barbarian Utopia" against the encroachments of cities.

Later in the meeting, MacKaye, Welch, and Perkins got together to discuss ATC business. Welch's work in park, camp, and highway development was increasing, not only in his New York job but also as a consultant to public figures from presidents to industrialists and to domestic and foreign park experts. A man who reputedly refused all news interviews (in sharp contrast to MacKaye), Welch wanted to relinquish an active ATC role. At the same time, Perkins wanted to retire from his family law firm, today still the oldest U.S. firm. As a result, Perkins informally took over the conference chairmanship and the vacuum that was its day-to-day leadership—informally, but vigorously. In what little of his correspondence and writings remain, his enthusiasm for all things A.T. and complete involvement in the project is infectious.

He spent his own money on the project, paying for MacKaye's travel to various meetings and "evolving," and paying for, what became one of the Trail's most enduring talismans. The A.T. monogram that Welch had devised and the pioneers approved as an emblem in October 1923 had in the ensuing four years been shifted from copper to aluminum, with embossed letters painted white. Within two years after Perkins took over, it was adopted as the official Trail emblem, and the copper square—with the painted monogram surrounded later by "Appalachian Trail—Maine to Georgia"—became a four-inch galvanized-iron square.

That shift, and the shift to a diamond shape after 1930, may have been simply a production decision, because the judge became a purchasing agent as well, succeeded in that role, too, by Avery. Perkins reported in the late 1920s that he had found a shop in downtown Hartford to produce them at the rate of 648 per sheet. Avery was procuring them by the hundreds, from Welch, Perkins, and the New York–New Jersey club. He apparently liked to nail them up about every 300 feet.

ABOVE: Acting ATC Chairman Arthur Perkins nails a sign similar to the ones on the next page to mark a recently scouted section of the A.T. in Maine in 1927.

In an October 1942 memoir in the Potomac Appalachian Trail Club's Bulletin, the club's supervisor of trails, J.P. Schairer, who had worked on the A.T. virtually from the beginning, recalled what those early weekends were like. Here are excerpts:

"Andy [H.C. Anderson] called me and said there was a fellow named Avery and [his uncle] Judge Cox and that the four of us would go to the mountains. We would take the Paris bus, and Andy and I would go south, and Myron and Judge Cox would go north. Then we would report on how the situation was—how hard it would be to cut a trail. None of us knew anything about it, and we had a terrible time finding our way. Andy and I had a topographic map, a lot of ambition, and lunch. Anyway, when we got together again, Andy and I reported that it was going to be a tough job to cut a trail. Myron and Judge Cox said there would be nothing to it . . . [I]t took several months of week-ends to get even a narrow trail cut . . .

"The thing which no one today can understand is how really difficult it was back in 1928 to get to the Blue Ridge and how much of an unknown land it was . . .

"On our first real work trip, Andy, Myron, and I took a train to Harpers Ferry. There was a bridge across in those days. We had to learn from sad experience how canteens are needed in the Blue Ridge, and we didn't have the kind of tools used today—clippers and weeders. We learned our trail technique the hard way. We used, that day, mainly Boy Scout axes. We were all dying of thirst after getting to the top. It took us all day to get from south of Chimney Rock to a point about half-mile beyond. Our axes got so dull we couldn't cut with them—we just had to saw off the twigs. When it came to Trail markers, we had a few copper ones that Major Welch had made at Bear Mountain and had given to us as his contribution to getting started. [Dr. P.L.] Ricker's idea was that we needed something to mark turns, so we bought those little wooden garden labels—little slats an inch wide and a foot-and-a-half long or so. Ricker printed on them 'Appalachian Trail' or 'Spring' or 'Viewpoint.' They solved the problem of marking the turns."

Volunteers' Trail signs from the late 1920s

TO SPRING

A. M. C. APPALACHIAN TRAIL. Conn. Chapter

APPALACHIAN TRAIL BLUE RIDGE SECTION

MYRON H. AVERY AND THE POTOMAC APPALACHIAN TRAIL CLUB

Myron H. Avery may or may not have been an intern during law school at Perkins's family firm (no documents have been found to prove or disprove stories Avery told of an 18-month "close association" in Hartford before going to Washington). Regardless, after receiving his law degree in 1923, he moved to Washington to take a job with what eventually became the U.S. Maritime Commission.

A native of Lubec, Maine, where his family was in the sardine-packing business, and a Phi Beta Kappa graduate of Bowdoin College before going to Harvard, he loved the outdoors from childhood and was a natural leader. While at Bowdoin during World War I, he even saw brief, nominal military service—basically, officer training.

About the time Perkins was moving into the lead of the Appalachian Trail project in New England, Avery, who had been hiking with a number of Washington-area outdoors clubs, heard about the Trail proposal and wrote Perkins to volunteer. With seven others, he organized the Potomac Appalachian Trail Club (PATC) in 1927 and was elected its first president. The mid-Atlantic states would become his first focus, although he and Raymond Torrey were both concerned about and working out routes for Pennsylvania.

Before Myron Avery and his group of friends had even founded the PATC, they had spent several weekends in northern Virginia, scouting and tentatively marking A.T. routes, and Avery was writing to Perkins for those permanent markers and guidance on to whom to report progress.

"While I haven't any authority to say so, not being an officer of the General Appalachian Trail Committee, I seem to be the one most interested," Perkins wrote back, "and, if you want to report directly to me, I will be glad to keep in touch with Major Welch or anybody else interested." Soon, Avery was urging Welch to call a second ATC meeting, and, by the following February, he was more than hinting that a return to Washington was fitting after three years: PATC was less than six months old, had about 40 members and $25 in the bank, and had blazed many miles of new trail already.

That was quickly settled. PATC would sponsor the meeting, Avery would keep the agenda focused on organizational issues, and he and Perkins would see to it that the project moved from the hands of talkers into the hands of doers. Out of the more than 200 people invited, only 28 people attended. The invitees included a proposed "Committee of 100" that looked like a directory of Washington at the time, with a few prominent New Yorkers thrown in—just the list an enterprising nonprofit fund-raiser would start with today. MacKaye did not attend the meeting, which featured a $2.50 dinner and a $3.50 round-trip bus ride to view new PATC trail about 60 miles to the west.

The meeting essentially was a series of appointments to committees—on a new constitution, on trail markers, on finances—and a reorganization of the ATC, a still-loose federation, including the institution of a 16-member board of managers, with a smaller executive committee. Welch was elected honorary chairman; Perkins, chairman and trail supervisor; J. Ashton Allis, treasurer. Avery, commissioned about this time as an officer in the Navy Reserve, was named to both the board and the executive committee.

ABOVE: Myron H. Avery, the longest-serving ATC chairman, took copious notes—for guidebooks, sign inventories, and his inspection reports—whenever he went to the Trail.

The reworded purpose of the organization was to "promote, establish and maintain a continuous trail for walkers, with a system of shelters and other necessary equipment . . . as a means for stimulating public interest in the protection, conservation and best use of the natural resources within" the mountains and wilderness areas of the East. About 500 miles of Trail, not all marked, were declared at least open for travel—primarily the existing links of the New England clubs and the New York–New Jersey Trail Conference.

MacKaye joined Perkins—and perhaps Avery—on two of the judge's many scouting trips for the Trail between Katahdin and the Potomac and attended club meetings in New England, too. Conference scrapbooks from this period already refer to the 50-ish writer as "our Nestor" (the wise old counselor of Homer's *Iliad* and *Odyssey*).

Many scouting trips were not refined. For many, getting to the mountains often meant a train or bus ride. If someone did happen to be among the less than 20 percent of Americans who owned an automobile, the roads from city to mountain—to the extent they existed at all for vehicles—were winding and unmaintained. When the blazers got to a crest where no established hiking trails existed to be brought into the proposed A.T., they went after roads abandoned by loggers and others who had worked the mountains to the bone in earlier eras. Next were woods roads still favored by hunters and other outdoorsmen, or, failing those, deer trails—or, as one witty early volunteer put it, "maybe the best-looking rabbit path we could see." The trips were generally short and definitely not without their adventures.

At the Conference's general meeting in May 1929, in Easton, Pennsylvania, further Avery-drafted revisions were made to the constitution, the absent Welch's title was changed to honorary president, and MacKaye spoke again on "The Origin and Conception of the A.T." The sign-in sheet is a priceless set of autographs of the A.T. founders, missing only Welch. Also speaking were John Finley, editor of *The New York Times* and honorary president of a Pennsylvania hiking club, and future U.S. Rep. Daniel Hoch, a club leader and future ATC board member who would play a key role in a later phase of the project while in Congress. This gathering proved to be the dividing line in the Appalachian Trail project—between the time of parlor talk and planning and the time of intense, in-the-field trailwork.

It was a dividing line in a small clan's remote world, though. In less than six months, the stock market would lose in five days the equivalent of 10 years of federal spending, not to recover its September peak for 20 years. The general economy would take less than half that time to recover, but not without another blow about the time the Trail would be finished. The Great Depression pushed the Roaring Twenties out the door. No hint of the country's or the world's turbulence survives in the Trail's archives. Avery did complain at some length, however, in his 1929 report about the historic chestnut blight—the loss of the giant trees on the southern mountains, after all, opened up the canopy and fueled weedy growth that kept obliterating his trail. The blight also destroyed a significant part of the unmentioned mountain economy and culture that those trailblazers would be heading toward.

ABOVE: In their only known photograph together, Benton MacKaye and Myron Avery pose at Bake Oven Knob in October 1931.
OPPOSITE: The sign-in sheet for the 1929 ATC meeting is a roster of most of the A.T. pioneers.

Arteur Perkins.

Marian E. Lapp

Eugene C. Bingham

Murray H. Stevens

Myron H. Avery – P.A.T.C.

Wm. J. Cooper, Blair Co Chapter, P.A.T.C.

H. F. Rentschler

J. Bruce Byall

Benton MacKaye

Frank Place. T+TCNY

P.J. Renner   Catskill Hiking Club N.Y. City

Mortimer Bishop – Mead. Air Club M.C.

C.P. Wilber – N.J. Dept. Conservation + Development.

A.M. Turner   Field Secretary, Conn. State Park + Forest Commission

Anna Rice Wilson

Katherine A. Erwin

Harold G. Anderson

Kathryn G. Fulkerson

Wm. F. Shanaman,

A.V. Parker.

Raymond H. Torrey.   Green Mountain Club, New York and Vermont
A. Bream Piper   Paterson Rambling Club
Penna Alpine Club   Torrey Botanical Club. N.Y. Chapter, Adirondack Mtn Club

Trail Towns

The Trail passes through or within five miles of 105 towns, more than two dozen of which have received ATC designation as an Appalachian Trail Community.

CHAPTER 2

Blazing the Footpath

I n late 1929, Judge Arthur Perkins estimated the total identified route for the A.T. as 1,300 miles, with about half of it "completed," a marked increase in just 18 months. Both estimates might have been a stretch.

In central Maine, Perkins had led the marking of a trail down Katahdin's Great South Basin in 1928, and it had been extended 20 miles to Moosehead Lake. As Myron Avery's era began, the AMC trails from Grafton Notch in Maine were doing double duty as the A.T., connecting to Dartmouth Outing Club trails from Mount Moosilauke west to reach the southern half of the Long Trail in Vermont, with only one three-mile gap. From Mount Greylock near the Massachusetts–Vermont border, a route to Mount Everett had been found, and existing trails were used to reach the Connecticut line. From there, individuals such as farmer Ned Anderson had marked a temporary route to the New York line near Kent, Connecticut, and old roads were followed from there to the Hudson River.

The pioneering New York–New Jersey crews had taken their trail from the original few miles at Bear Mountain out to Greenwood Lake just above the New Jersey line and reported the Garden State "almost done." The route across Pennsylvania atop Blue Mountain from the Delaware Water Gap to Harrisburg was called "available," while the Conference leaders continued to bat around

various ideas to take the A.T. from the Susquehanna River south to the Potomac River, Maryland's southern boundary.

Not waiting around for that decision, crews led by Avery had marked 100 miles from Harpers Ferry, West Virginia, on the Potomac, well into the proposed Shenandoah National Park. Crews in the Natural Bridge National Forest just to the south had laid down a route to the Peaks of Otter in central Virginia.

From there to Grandfather Mountain in northwestern North Carolina, the highest point on the Blue Ridge Range, and on toward the Georgia line, the core group was looking at the possibilities with more than a little disagreement between North Carolina and Tennessee trailblazers, not only about the passage across their states but also about where to put the southern terminus and whether or not to have "branch lines" as Benton MacKaye originally proposed. "This area is a present blank," Avery reported in Easton, Pennsylvania, in 1929.

It was a blank only in the sense that it lacked a decided route beyond general agreement that the new, largely unmapped and untraveled Great Smoky Mountains National Park should be included. The Smoky Mountains Hiking Club, about a year older than the ATC, was the only club south of Pennsylvania when the 1930s began, and the new park was its focus. Originally, working with the most general of maps, MacKaye had proposed running the Trail over Mount Mitchell in North Carolina, the East's highest peak, and then ending slightly to the southwest in the Cohutta Mountains of Georgia or perhaps Lookout Mountain just south of Chattanooga, Tennessee. South of Roanoke, Virginia, the Blue Ridge Range forks into two ranges that come together again at Springer Mountain in north Georgia, which is southeast of both of the early suggested termini.

Roy Ozmer, a Virginian who moved first to Tennessee and then Georgia by 1930, was recruited as an A.T. scout in 1928 and explored all the possibilities south of Shenandoah in 1929. (He had planned to walk all the way to Maine, blazing at least 700 miles as he went, but a back injury stopped him.) A hard driver not unlike Avery, he quickly teamed up with Everett (Eddie) B. Stone, an assistant Georgia state forester described by his own assistant as "slight of build and active as a mouse on store-bought cheese."

Stone was determined to have the Trail on the eastern wing of the Blue Ridge from the North Carolina line, bisecting the Cherokee National Forest (since renamed Chattahoochee) to Mount Oglethorpe, south of Springer Mountain. The owner of Oglethorpe at the time, Colonel Sam Tate, was developing a resort there and in the process of having the state legislature rename it from Grassy Mountain. (The next year, his family would underwrite the building of the first A.T. shelter in Georgia, complete with a fence to keep out wild hogs.)

According to *Friendships of the Trail*, the history of the Georgia Appalachian Trail Club (GATC), Stone believed that public forests should serve many interests, not just timbering, and that the Trail would bring many men and women to the forests for recreation, outdoors people who then would become advocates for the forests' many possible purposes.

Ozmer had nothing respectful to say about other routes through Georgia: "I felt the only logical, appropriate, and *humane* place for the southern terminus was Oglethorpe." From the

PREVIOUS SPREAD: In the Virginia woods.
ABOVE: Myron Avery leads Potomac Appalachian Trail Club and Maine Appalachian Trail Club volunteers above the treeline on Katahdin to mount the first sign at the northern terminus in 1935.
OPPOSITE: One of the scores of USGS quadrangle maps Avery annotated while plotting and measuring Trail routes.

THE APPALACHIAN TRAIL

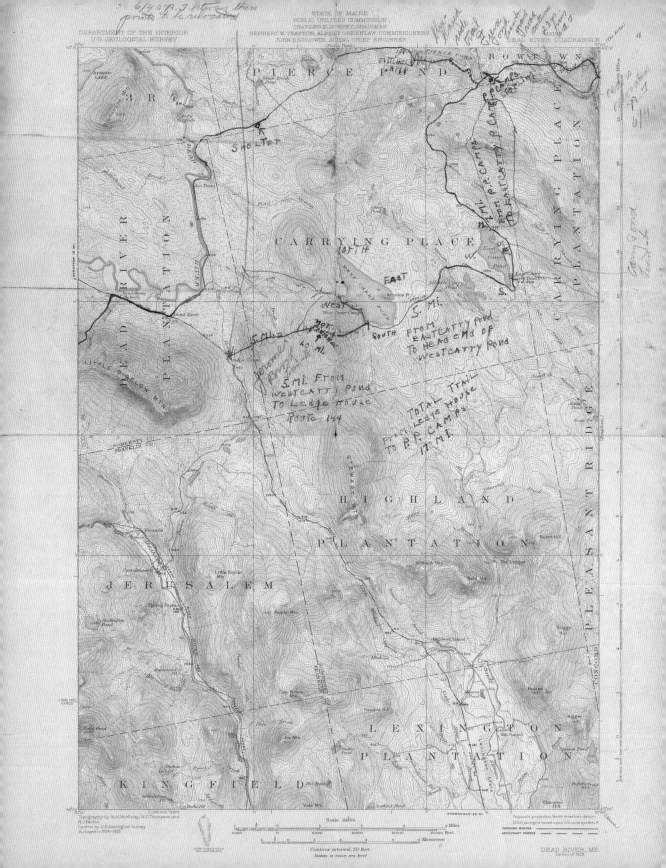

STATE OF MAINE
PUBLIC UTILITIES COMMISSION
CHARLES E. GURNEY, CHAIRMAN
HERBERT W. TRAFTON, ALBERT GREENLAW, COMMISSIONERS
JOHN E. GOODWIN, ACTING CHIEF ENGINEER

DEPARTMENT OF THE INTERIOR
U.S. GEOLOGICAL SURVEY

DEAD RIVER QUADRANGLE
MAINE

DEAD RIVER, ME.
Edition of 1929

Topography by W.K.McKinley, W.C.Thompson, and R.J.Belton
Control by U.S.Geological Survey
Surveyed in 1924-1925

Scale 62500

Contour interval 20 feet
Datum is mean sea level

O-5184

Georgia boundary, he wanted the route to take a more or less straight course to the middle of the proposed Smokies park. A faction in the Smokies club had a different idea, though: stay in the western fork (of which the Smoky Mountains were part) and head toward the Cohuttas in Georgia, just south of the Tennessee line.

The previous summer, Avery had written Perkins, detailing all sorts of geological, forest-service, and trailblazers' arguments, noting that the Trail project had no interested believers in the Cohutta area and concluding: "No one of us know that country, and I think in the final analysis we should be governed by the views of [Paul] Fink and Ozmer . . . . Let's at least finish the southern end while we can."

Stone did not wait for the approval of outsiders, especially northerners who had never even visited. He set about blazing and marking *his* route. Perkins, when asked, said nothing official had been decided, and Stone was furious, writing back to Perkins his views and noting that he had an Oglethorpe dedication planned for May 1930. Horace Kephart, the most respected outdoors writer of his day and a leader of the push for the Smokies park as well as the A.T., reinforced Stone and Ozmer for Georgia, although his proposed route across North Carolina would be more of a zigzag toward the Tennessee line than Ozmer was suggesting. Kephart's letter was dated February 21. Neither he nor most others in the project knew that a few weeks earlier Perkins had suffered the first of what would be a series of strokes—"shocks" was the term Perkins used.

All the activists continued writing each other frequently, trading reports on routes and planning the next ATC meeting (May 30–31) at Skyland in Shenandoah Park. Making Mount Oglethorpe the official southern terminus would be the main business, since the Smokies club had accepted the Kephart compromise in March. It required a Conference vote and received a unanimous one, helped immeasurably by a display of images presented by Japanese-American photographer George Masa, Kephart's partner in hiking, A.T. scouting, and park advocacy.

After another stroke in April, Perkins asked Avery to take full charge over the upcoming meeting, although Major William Welch, the honorary chairman, went down to preside, as he did for several more meetings, and MacKaye attended as well. Three days before the meeting, Perkins wrote Avery to say he continued to have dizzy spells, losing his vision occasionally and suffering "intense nausea."

At the meeting itself—about half meeting and half hiking, riding, or socializing among the 198 attendees—MacKaye gave a rambling speech, in which he foreshadowed the position that soon would put him and a few friends at loggerheads with the emerging ATC leadership. Adding "simple sanitation facilities" to the "primeval" Trail might be acceptable, "but anything of sight or sound or other human sensibility which injects unneeded the metropolitan influence is a distinct trespass . . . and hence a defeat of the whole purpose of any project, like the Appalachian Trail, for preserving this realm . . . . *To preserve the primeval environment*: This is the point, the whole point, and nothing but the point of the Appalachian Trail."

Three weeks after the Skyland meeting, Perkins wrote to Avery: "I hope you are going to help me out . . . . What I would like most would be to have you assume the title of Acting Chairman, as I

OPPOSITE: Renowned Southern writer (and ATC board member) Horace Kephart, while scouting A.T. routes in the valleys, inspects a marker from the 1860s Cataloochee Turnpike, the first wagon road in the Smokies, which closely followed much older Cherokee hunting trails.

did when Major Welch could not attend to things, though for another reason, and give as much time as you reasonably can to Trail interests." Judge Perkins officially remained chairman until the 1931 meeting, with honorary titles thereafter until his death in May 1932 on his 68th birthday.

THE REIGN OF MYRON AVERY

Avery, with his dual ATC/PATC positions and phenomenal dedication to the cause, set about indefatigably recruiting volunteers, organizing clubs, plotting routes—and flagging and cutting and constructing and blazing and measuring them—and writing construction manuals and guidebooks. He published them with his own money at first or with funds from Jean Stephenson, probably his closest associate in the project.

Out of his practical experience (and those of clubs he encouraged) and his natural inclination toward instruction and imposed standards, Avery even in the early 1930s phased out the metal markers he once could not get enough of in favor of the painted white blaze that is the A.T.'s signature today (borrowed from the original Long Trail in Vermont). But, make no mistake: It was to be "six inches long and two inches wide (no more) made at the height of the eye," with no deviations. Avery spent hours testing various formulas for white paint that were just right for the Trail in all regions and seasons. As a practical matter, both markers and blazes lined the route for some time, in part because the A.T. "borrowed" other trails throughout New England especially, so blazes of other colors needed to be linked with the metal markers to guide hikers.

It is worth remembering that the most active of the A.T. activists, such as Avery and Eddie Stone, held full-time professional jobs. The Washington squad routinely went from those jobs to full evenings at makeshift offices to work on Trail business during the week, and then out to the mountains for the weekends.

Avery already cut an iconic figure in the field—small notebook and pencil in one hand to note every sign and landmark and "the Wheel" in the other. Loaned to him in 1928 or 1929 by the Appalachian Mountain Club, the front of a bicycle with a makeshift handle and a cyclometer attached to the wheel would become his hallmark forever. After the 1930 ATC meeting, he backpacked 70 miles in three days in central Virginia, measuring as he went, and wrote Perkins of his excitement: "When we climbed the Peaks of Otter, we would see the route of the Trail along the Blue Ridge to a point near Roanoke."

In the office, he was no less energetic, dictating 40 letters on Trail matters one night and 20 more the next. After two or three evenings of working until midnight on dictations, he took those who typed the letters "out to a sumptuous dinner at a quality restaurant," the club's history reports. Many of those letters to local clubs, game wardens, district rangers, or board members were basically long ways of chiding for not having this or that done yet. Completion of the continuous footpath—primarily for solitary hiking—became Avery's main goal within the organization.

A history of the PATC by David Bates, *Breaking Trail in the Central Appalachians*, said of Perkins's young protégé, "Myron Avery kept a very firm hand on all activities within the PATC . . . .

ABOVE: Myron Avery demonstrates a soon-abandoned technique for scraping off bark before painting blazes in the 1930s.
OPPOSITE: Pioneer maintainer William F. Etchberger took this photograph of Avery during a measuring trip for the relocation at Indiantown Gap, Pennsylvania.

He followed all projects in detail, often calling or writing to committee chairmen to keep in touch or prod them along. He often planned the trips . . . in every detail." Avery handled public relations, wrote newspaper articles, and dealt with the federal agencies—all as a volunteer. There was no paid staff, and Avery's writings later were forceful in advocating a totally volunteer A.T. effort.

"He could be, and sometimes was, arbitrary and abrasive," Bates wrote, "but more often he was understanding, considerate and helpful, and had a good sense of humor . . . . [In] view of what was accomplished under his leadership, members should be grateful that the club had this man at its head, whether he was 'one-way' or not."

"When I think of my father," Avery's surviving son, Hal, told the *Appalachian Trailway News* in 2000, "I think of his characteristics—I think of a very ethical, very moral man, quite demanding of all of us, almost on a perfectionist level. And, he was equally demanding of himself."

Avery's clubmates directly poked fun at "Emperor Myronides I" and—if close enough, such as Stephenson—occasionally berated him (in writing) for his imperial tone. Bill Mersch, a bus driver for the PATC who became trails supervisor in the 1940s, is quoted by Larry Luxenberg, author of the standard history of A.T. thru-hiking, as saying, "Myron left two trails from Maine to Georgia. One was of hurt feelings and bruised egos. The other was the A.T."

"Avery was the right man for the times," Luxenberg quoted David B. Field, a Maine forestry professor, descendant of the first white man known to climb Mount Washington, A.T. maintainer since the mid-1950s, and former ATC chairman himself. "The difficulties facing the Conference absolutely demanded strong and even autocratic leadership. It was the only way it could have gotten done. Avery made a lot of friends and a lot of enemies. He was what it required at the time, not just for Maine but for the whole Trail."

Whether or not Avery was a difficult personality is, of course, subjective. The fact remains that PATC trips during the organization's first four years resulted in the cutting of some 265 miles of Trail from central Pennsylvania to central Virginia and a whole string of new A.T. clubs south of Harpers Ferry into North Carolina, which was crucial to the completion of the Trail. MacKaye later praised "this vigorous club [as] a maker of clubs."

Much of this southern Appalachian territory that Perkins, Avery, Halstead Hedges, Paul Fink, and others charted for the A.T. was truly isolated backcountry, physically and culturally. Memoirs of some ATC pioneers say they weren't even sure exactly where the Appalachians ended in the South. The federal government had not yet officially mapped some of these areas topographically, and what residents this wilderness had were highly suspicious of those who penetrated its hollows and ridges. In the course of his scouting, Avery learned that Swiss-American geographer Arnold H. Guyot had indeed mapped many parts of potential Trail routes in the South in the mid-19th century. He found Guyot's papers in the National Archives, published them under the ATC imprint, and then used them to help chart a footpath.

WILDERNESS VS. ACCESS

In 1931, with 1,207 miles of an estimated 1,300-mile Appalachian Trail completed, Avery was officially elected ATC chairman, a position he would hold for the next 21 years. Yet, even before the meeting at which he was first elected, an internal battle that would alternately plague and nag the Trail project for decades was not-so-quietly brewing.

The lack of road access to the mountains that so frustrated and delayed the early trailblazers was soon to be "remedied"—to the detriment of the Trail in most minds. More and better roads *would* make it easier both to make and hike trails. Officials of and advocates for new national forests and parks needed roads to attract the public to their lands—a public they counted on to support maintenance funds for those forests and parks. Indeed, research cited by Tim Cole for his history degree from the University of North Carolina at Asheville "indicated that places like Great Smoky Mountains National Park were established due to automobiles and roads rather than the transcendental qualities of nature."

It made for some family spats. In Georgia, for example, Forest Supervisor Clinton Smith, an original 1925 ATC executive-committee member, had a comprehensive plan for roads—some of which would have obliterated the Georgia A.T. that had just been completely marked in February. Arthur Woody, a now-legendary district "barefoot ranger" along the southern end of

OPPOSITE: From the expressions of his hiker audience, it could have been one of his trailside "sermons," but Myron Avery always appears as the leader in group photographs from his era.

the Trail known for restoring wildlife, wanted roads across "his" mountain passes (and he did own a lot of the land).

The GATC rose up to fight all of these road plans and reached out to MacKaye and his friends and to Avery for help. Eventually, most "crestline" roads were abandoned in favor of "flankline" roads paralleling the Trail, but passes were being paved and relocations being forced here and there. It became a constant wilderness-versus-access issue in Trail-project correspondence, with Avery tending toward supporting the feelings of local clubs—whether to fight or compromise—and those around MacKaye growing in anger, opposing all mountain roads.

To secure a more direct feel for both the rugged terrain there and the issues, Avery went south to meet the charismatic new president of the Georgia club, a local newspaper publisher named Warner Hall. They hiked from Georgia to the annual ATC meeting in Gatlinburg, Tennessee, more than 200 miles away, prompting extraordinary local newspaper publicity when they arrived and for the duration of the three-day conference. At that conference, 177 delegates and almost 75 guests listened as Paul Fink proclaimed the Trail "almost completed":

> Sixty percent of the trail is marked, and trail data are available, though it is not yet possible to follow the A.T. markers from Mt. Oglethorpe to Mt. Katahdin. The two factors which enlisted interest in the Trail were the characteristics of the American people to carry out a big idea that requires a great deal of work to do, and the absolute democracy of the Appalachian Trail idea, which brings all together with the common interest of making the dream of Benton MacKaye a reality.

MacKaye was not present at this meeting, but Harvey Broome of the host Smokies club, who some would call MacKaye's surrogate son, read his message, in which he expanded on his themes from the previous year in a bit harsher fashion: "Our job is to make an American sanctuary—for the birds and the trees, yes, and through them for *ourselves*: to do this in a particular place, namely the great central primeval barrier of the Appalachian Mountains."

He went on to list three ways not to use the Trail: "Not as a race course . . . . Keep athletics in their place! The contact on the Trail is that of man to nature . . . . Not as a make-believe. Let no corner of our primeval world sink to the order of an 'amusement park,'" aspects of which he cited radios, motion pictures, and motor cars. And, "not in any way as a deflection of our aims . . . . No trespassing in any form or manner of the metropolitan influence as such."

MacKaye concluded by calling, in the footpath's second decade, for a physical expansion of the Trail estate "to square miles of public reservation" and expansion "of the knowledge (and the feeling) of primeval history . . . . The pioneers of the 1830s opened the wilderness to a passing civilization; and you, the pioneers of the 1930s, will open civilization to the eternal wilderness."

At this time, MacKaye considered the Trail firmly established, and the following year wrote for *The Scientific Monthly* what he called a sequel to his seminal 1921 article. It was the answer, he said, to "the question so often put to me by J.P. [Judge Perkins]: 'When we get the Trail, Ben, what are we going to do with it?'" In "The Appalachian Trail: A Guide to the Study of Nature," he reiterated his position

OPPOSITE: In one of the most rugged Trail sections south of New Hampshire, pioneer E. Guy Frizzell steadies a sign for the path off the road at what is now called Stecoah Gap in southwestern North Carolina between the Nantahala River and the Smokies park.

that trail-building was and should be only the "first long step in the longer pursuit of becoming harmonized with scenery—and the primeval influence—the opposite of machine influence." He declared the project to be in its second stage: development of a primeval understanding.

Avery, on the other hand, promoted both trail-building and hiking as essential keys to instilling individual resourcefulness and protection of the footpath itself against development. He was moving the Conference in a different direction, narrowing the focus of the organization's stated intent, redefining the purposes of the project, and reinterpreting its history as he went.

In a 1930 article in *Mountain Magazine*, then the project's principal outlet to its enthusiasts, Avery—who was as prolific a writer as he was an industrious Trail scout—began flatly: "The Appalachian Trail, *as conceived* by its proponents and already partly realized, is a *footpath for hikers* in the Appalachian Mountains, extending from Maine to Georgia, a distance of some 1,300 miles." (Emphasis added.) Access to the mountains for "tramping, camping, and outdoor recreation" was the Trail's purpose.

MacKaye was mentioned only once in Avery's article and not listed on the ATC "membership" roster of 11 public officials, 16 clubs, and the New Jersey High Park Commission that concluded the piece—a decline from the 207 officials and organizations Perkins cited at the end of the 1920s.

THE DEPRESSION'S EFFECTS: 1932–1934

Away from public print on the project, the Depression was having its effect and things were slowing down, although these facts were more between the lines than obvious in project documents. Clubs were sponsoring group hikes where sections were finished, including the Smokies— reporting on flora and fauna and accomplishments small and large, such as finding the source of the Chattahoochee River, which provides water to all of Atlanta, Georgia, to the south. The 1932 meeting at the Long Trail Inn on the crest of the Green Mountains east of Rutland, Vermont, was postponed into 1933, however—ostensibly for lack of enough to talk about—and then again into 1934, because of the "financial embarrassments" of members. Avery asked for $15 from all member clubs and organizations to defray costs of markers, office supplies, and other operating expenses—and it took a year to get enough, usually in $10 increments. This amount was not insignificant: $10 then would be more than $167 today; the ATC had a $585 budget.

By 1933, the U.S. Forest Service and the southern clubs, initially predicted to be the probable last ones to finish, reported their third of the Trail essentially completed. That third was primarily within national forests (and the Smokies park), and a pattern had developed: Clubs would scout and blaze, and forest crews would build to their standards, erect shelters, and maintain the footpath while clubs maintained markers, blazes, and guides. (It would not be until the late 1990s that a larger management role for the clubs distinct from the agencies would be agreed to and put on paper.)

By that time, it was only the Trail in Maine, rather than the South, that still seemed an impossible dream. Conference leaders considered withdrawing the northern terminus to the original Mount Washington point. Avery resisted any desertion of the planned route through his native

OPPOSITE: Hiking ties were gone by the 1950s, but fedoras were still hanging on.

Maine and initiated an intensive survey of remote areas planned for the Trail and scouted earlier. That reinforced the local efforts of such men as Walter D. Greene, a Broadway actor, and Helon N. Taylor, then a husky, fit game warden and later supervisor of Baxter State Park (home of Katahdin).

The fun-loving GATC, in the absence of an all-Trail meeting in 1933, organized its own for all the southern clubs, at which a lifelong bond was formed between it and MacKaye. Although he then was working in Knoxville, Tennessee, for the new, quasigovernmental Tennessee Valley Authority, in a letter to a club leader after the meeting, he warned of the dangers of clubs being diverted from the true cause by becoming too close to government, especially in seeking federal funds. "If the government spends money, it demands—reasonably enough—to have 'something to show for it . . . . ' If it is something merely physical, then it must be very physical—and the tendency will be to manicure the wilderness. This is the opposite concept of the Appalachian Trail," he wrote.

Work in every state now moved rapidly. By 1934, clubs reported completion of 1,937 miles of Trail. In Georgia, another icon was created. Dr. George H. Noble, an amateur sculptor, crafted three bronze plaques signifying the Trail with the inscription, "A Footpath for Those Who Seek Fellowship with the Wilderness." One was mounted at Mount Oglethorpe, but no one had funds to erect the other two.

"Our original purpose . . . was to give added prestige to the Appalachian Trail in our section . . . " Warner Hall, who had posed for it, wrote of the plaque that May. "Local forest and park authorities, who had looked upon our activities as rather juvenile and the Trail as unimportant, are asking us to tell them more about this Trail which deserves such an elaborate marker." Today, its bluish-green patina marks the first step northbound atop Springer Mountain.

When the full Conference did finally meet in Vermont in 1934, the fissure among the founding fathers became clearer and more public. The MacKaye-centric element publicly led by Raymond Torrey and H.C. Anderson first questioned who the ATC's members were and which had how many votes. Avery responded that, actually, the ATC had no members because membership had never been defined in the 1929 constitution; therefore, constitutional amendments on the issue would be in order for the next meeting, which would be hosted by the PATC. MacKaye's supporters then tried to raise the issue of "skyline drives," to oppose them in all instances (except in Shenandoah National Park, a *fait accompli*).

They failed. As Anderson later wrote MacKaye, "I am certainly not in sympathy with the pusillanimous, Lazarus-like attitude of some of the leaders of the Conference. You and Bob Marshall have been preaching that those who love the primitive should get together and give a united expression of their views. That is what I would like to get started." He received his wish.

That October, somewhere outside of Knoxville, Tennessee, their car—yes—"came to a screeching halt" and MacKaye, Broome, and two other occupants got out to sit on an embankment to argue over "a handwritten draft of a constitution for a new conservation group," according to its Internet site today. The following January, MacKaye, Harvey Broome, Bob Marshall (chief of lands and recreation for the Forest Service), Anderson, Aldo Leopold, Robert Sterling Yard

ABOVE AND OPPOSITE: Georgia Appalachian Trail Club President Warner Hall poses for the classic George Noble bronze plaque that now marks hikers' first northbound steps on the Appalachian Trail atop Springer Mountain, Georgia.

(National Park Service publicist), Bernard Frank, and Ernest Oberholtzer incorporated The Wilderness Society. Paul Fink, who previously had tried to mediate quarrels between different passionate groups, termed their prospectus "a little rabid" and in the fall told Avery he agreed they were having a toxic effect.

A TURNING POINT: FLANKLINE VS. SKYLINE

In June 1935, the Maine Appalachian Trail Club (MATC) was formed, with heavy PATC involvement and inspiration (including Avery as its overseer of trails from 1935 to 1949 and its president from 1949 until his death in 1952). Members traveled from Washington, D.C., in the summer months for the work trips that got the larger parts of the Trail finished. With ATC help and the encouragement of state and federal forest services, the Appalachian Trail—primarily in Maine and

THE APPALACHIAN TRAIL

the southern states—became an item on the agenda of the Depression-era Civilian Conservation Corps (CCC), which was formed in 1933. Several of those crews set standards of trail-construction quality that have yet to be surpassed. It was a mixed blessing for the Trail, though. The CCC also had a road-building agenda, which the GATC had been alternately discovering (by seeing survey flags when they hiked) and battling for more than a year.

The year 1935 also marked a less positive turning point in the Trail project's history, one that, as noted earlier, had been coming for several years. The immediate point of contention was the federal government's work-in-progress to construct with CCC labor the Skyline Drive through Virginia, which was essentially right on top of the Appalachian Trail in the centerpiece of Avery's PATC section.

Avery and other PATC and ATC leaders—if not a majority, certainly a controlling faction—felt that they needed government allies to further the values of the Trail as a whole for the long-term future. Federal resources agencies had been involved with the A.T. project virtually from its start. Avery's circle also sensed that the backers of this scenic highway had more political clout than they did. They chose not to fight it, opting instead for cooperative relocation of the Trail (accomplished largely by CCC crews at government expense, as it turned out, without a break in the route). That new, graded trail was under construction and promptly labeled a sidewalk by critics.

Others in both organizations wanted to fight the construction of Skyline Drive as an intrusion on the wilderness and a threat to the Trail as it was conceived. Most opponents seemed to be in MacKaye's circle of associates, including Raymond Torrey in New York, Harvey Broome in Tennessee, and H.C. Anderson at PATC. Broome's club, the Smoky Mountains Hiking Club, and the Appalachian Mountain Club (AMC)—then and now the largest of the confederated clubs in the project—took positions against the roadway's construction.

In an article the AMC asked him to write for its *Appalachia* magazine and then reprinted for wider distribution, "Flankline vs. Skyline," MacKaye had strongly attacked the idea of skyline drives, in Virginia and elsewhere. He asserted that neither campers nor motorists nor "frolickers" ("young souls who should be confined to outing areas" away from wilderness) wanted such roadways, only salesmen, "persons who (as hotel-keepers, food-vendors, or contractors) hope to capitalize the wilderness by means of selling something." He proposed scenic routes along the mountains' flanks as a solution ideal for all, but conceded that "the salesmen and contractors" already had an enormous marketing advantage for "their" idea. Other critics suggested limiting highway funds to improving or initiating valley roads that would serve more people in need.

Torrey, Anderson, and others prepared and circulated—but did not submit according to the rules—a resolution for the June 1935 ATC meeting at Skyland opposing skyline drives interfering with the A.T. and government-constructed trails. Avery, whose chairman's report focused entirely on the need for more and better maintenance, prepared and submitted according to his rules a resolution that basically said such road proposals should be considered on their merits and as locally as feasible. It is easy to assume Avery made sure he had the votes. Both resolutions brought a flurry of mail to the ATC in Washington before the meeting.

OPPOSITE: Trailside waterfalls, like this one in Virginia, provide not only relief from thirst and heat but also visual highlights of the regenerating eastern forests.

The AMC's Brooklyn-based editor at the time, R. G. Hardy, wrote, "'A footpath in the wilderness' cannot well become an adjunct to a highway and retain its original character . . . . The whole character of such a trail project as ours can only be maintained if it continues to be an amateur undertaking, kept up for the love of walking and the out-of-doors. As soon as any such project is taken over by the government . . . it is liable to be too fussily taken care of, too much advertised, too well guarded against the true wilderness spirit."

Both the "modern, spic and span parks" and associated roads will lead to noise, vandalism, loss of wildlife, and destruction of remaining wilderness, wrote H. A. Allard from his Agriculture Department office. "We have displaced the native mountaineer to move in by hordes a tourist population."

Anderson also circulated his interpretation of ATC "membership"—not following the procedures for amendments—while Avery prepared detailed constitutional amendments, backed by parliamentary-law citations, defining membership. His faction not so incidentally noted that a category for individual memberships at $5 per person would bring in much-needed revenue.

At the meeting, with apparently half the attendees or "delegates" from the PATC, Torrey was not reelected treasurer, Anderson was not reelected to the board, and Avery's membership definitions were adopted 78–8. Then, Torrey had to be goaded into moving his resolution from the floor but did not speak for it. After some extended back-and-forth over whether some of Torrey's language was insulting to the National Park Service, Avery's roads resolution was substituted. (Torrey said he had no objection to what he later called a "spineless" position.) It was adopted by unanimous voice vote without further discussion.

In a written message read by Broome the night before, MacKaye had sounded his position that the purpose of the project transcended the miracle of constructing the Trail: "The mere footpath is no end in itself, but a means of sojourning in the wilderness, whose nurture is your particular care." As he had written in 1930, he felt that the purpose of the Appalachian Trail should be "to extend the primeval environment and to set bounds to the metropolitan environment."

In fewer than four months following the meeting, Torrey published 11 "Long Brown Path" columns in *The New York Post* denouncing the results of the meeting regarding skyline highways and denouncing "the Avery outfit" or PATC domination of the ATC. At the end of October, Avery started to write publicly about a preserve to protect the Trail, and MacKaye left his regional planning job at the Tennessee Valley Authority to return to Massachusetts. Jean Stephenson and three other PATC officers fired back at Torrey with their own 21-page "statement of facts," printed for mass distribution. They concluded that the columns were not only erroneous, but also brought disrepute, disunity, and dissension within the Trail project. (Interestingly, Torrey, although a Wilderness Society "representative" in New York, was back at the podium within two years, supporting Avery positions as president of the New York–New Jersey Trail Conference.)

In December, Avery went to the presumed source. In response to some materials on the issue Avery had sent earlier in the month, MacKaye had written to him on November 20, repeating his attacks on skyline roads. His letter accused Avery of a "connectivitis" ailment—

pushing to complete the Trail at all costs—and, Avery inferred, "assigns to me a point of view and then proceeds to demolish it." Early in his six-page response, dated December 19 but not mailed until December 30, Avery wrote, "You will have to take full responsibility for this diagnosis; it is your fantasy—nothing of mine." This response began with his normal, "My dear Benton," and continued in his sometimes oblique, sometimes Victorian prose to rebut point-by-point MacKaye's recent assertions about the Trail.

But first, Avery expressed "the greatest of regret . . . that he who had conceived the Appalachian Trail had consciously placed himself at the disposal of the elements which have attempted to wreck the project and prevent its completion . . . . [The] personal attacks, gross misrepresentation of facts, intolerance, and abuse which have, of late, been showered upon the active workers in the Trail project have disillusioned many . . . . I, for one, am thoroughly disillusioned and disgusted."

"I suspect that years and years from now, after we have followed our new technologies and grand urban schemes into a new century, the Trail will remain a sure route into our past, a route along which technology will always surrender to strength and spirit and the laws of nature . . . . My memories of the months on the Trail have survived as a time of sublime happiness, a time when I felt my neurons being switched on for the very first time. The mention of the Trail still evokes images of lush, green mountains; of great gray clouds of mist wafting through virgin stands of hemlock and oak; of bald-topped mountains with views that roll out across miles and miles of blue-hazed hills; of hawks swirling above sun-drenched granite ledges; of springs that run so cold they made my teeth ache . . . . I doubt that any other event of my life will choke me with as much emotion, fill me with as much pride, or define more clearly who I am than my summer on the Appalachian Trail."

—DAVID BRILL, 1990, *As Far as the Eye Can See*

As to the criticism of using CCC help, Avery wrote, "Had you ever worked on the Trail . . . you might well appreciate the reaction to such armchair suggestions . . . . I do wish those who talk so much about the 'footless' Trail and the 'wilderness' Trail would really go out on the Trail."

He went on to correctly say, in summary, that the lands crossed by the Appalachian Trail were not true wilderness and certainly not primeval and that, even if they were, a walker could appreciate nothing about the forest if he had to be constantly on guard against getting lost on an improperly marked and maintained footpath. Avery also implicitly criticized MacKaye for not sufficiently supporting the ATC and PATC in their attempts to work with the government as a partner, rather than take it on as an adversary. He detailed what he, Avery, had done for the Trail—in Shenandoah in particular—and what he, MacKaye, had not.

Near the end, he acknowledged the threats of roads and the need to act when it would do good, but "passing resolutions and everlastingly talking is of little use . . . . The obstructionist attitude merely creates antagonism in the mind of the public against the out-of-door groups. We are endeavoring to build not only a physical trail but to develop in the urban population the realization of the benefits to be obtained from seeking that Trail and following it. We can never create that feeling if we present a spectacle of fanaticism, selfishness, or intolerance."

Two months later, in February 1936, MacKaye wrote a letter reprimanding Avery for his "self-righteous, overbearing attitude and a bullying manner of expression." No researcher has found any evidence that these two men ever spoke or wrote to each other again in the 16 years before Avery died, but the last membership meeting over which Avery presided, in 1948, did award MacKaye a commemorative plaque, and MacKaye graciously thanked the Conference.

Those who have studied the break between MacKaye and Avery confirm that it had little or nothing to do with cooperating with the government. MacKaye, after all, had advocated total public ownership of Trail lands at least as far back as 1927. Instead, it was the result of radical differences in personal styles, strategies, and tactics and the fundamentally different philosophical concepts of what the Trail should be and become: a footpath as a first-class engineered entity and an end in itself *versus* a footpath as a mere means to a metaphysical end, with social and economic applications to hold back and reform the metropolis. MacKaye pushed for protecting wilderness as an environment for higher human evolution; he even opposed delegates "going by motor car" to the tense 1935 conference. Avery pushed for completion of the chosen task of making the mountains accessible for outdoor recreation.

In 1936, MacKaye turned much of his intellectual energy toward the Wilderness Society and, 10 years later, became its president. He did maintain inspiring correspondence with many compatible club and conference leaders, though, always writing fondly of the Conference and the Trail maintainers. (After Avery's death, chairmen and executives stayed in touch with MacKaye on a fairly regular basis, and he was awarded honorary membership in 1967.)

FROM MAINE TO GEORGIA: FINISHING THE TRAIL

The work of the Trail project went on, with Avery's energies unabated; Maine needed to be finished. Avery published a pamphlet calling the Trail there "the silver aisle," although more than half of it was on roads and such "paths" as forest-telephone rights-of-way. Judge Perkins in the mid-1920s and Arthur Comey—the New England Trail Conference leader who had been in MacKaye's circle at the beginning—in 1929 had scouted routes from the north end. But, it was Walter D. Greene, the Broadway actor, who singlehandedly carried the ball for Avery in the meantime. Greene—also a registered Maine guide who had a summer home in Sebic— met Avery by chance during an exploration north of Katahdin. He went on to blaze a route to Blanchard and then tackled the rugged Barren–Chairback Range section by section, with side trails to such wonders as Gulf Hagas.

ABOVE: Broadway actor Walter D. Greene singlehandedly scouted much of the initial Appalachian Trail in Maine until Myron Avery formed the Maine Appalachian Trail Club and enlisted local officials to finish the job.

Other guides, educators, and interested local residents were picking up more sections here and there—they all insisted it be a "homegrown" effort—with Avery leading a special expedition with his Washington friends in 1933. He recruited all manner of forces—railroad and paper companies, quarrymen, and the state forest service among them—to connect the more than 260 miles to the AMC's White Mountain trails that extended into Maine about 15 miles.

A continuous Appalachian Trail from Maine to Georgia should have been pronounced open, under Avery's schedule, in 1936. By that time, he had walked and measured every step of the scouted or constructed route and as such became the first "2,000-miler" on the footpath.

One mile remained between Davenport Gap and the Big Pigeon River in Tennessee, and two miles had to be built 186 miles south of Katahdin, on a high ridge connecting Spaulding and Sugarloaf mountains in Maine. A late-summer snowstorm prevented completion of the Maine work in 1936. With the southern gap in the 2,025-mile route taken care of early the next spring, a six-man CCC crew completed the final link in the Maine woods, without fanfare, on August 14, 1937. Leon P. Brooks, the foreman, advised Avery by letter two days later and noted they would be moving on to build shelters.

Two months earlier, Avery had quietly saluted the imminent completion of the Trail-construction era—saluting the Southern "conquerors" for beating his home-state alliance—but immediately challenged ATC members at the meeting in Gatlinburg, Tennessee:

> Rather than a sense of exultation, this situation brings a fuller realization of our responsibilities. To say that the Trail is completed would be a complete misnomer. Those of us, who have physically worked on the Trail, know that the Trail, as such, will never be completed. As long as the project exists, there will be ever present, in increasing seriousness, the problems of maintenance and of developing a greater utilization of the Trail's attractions. On this score, the Appalachian Trail will always be unfinished.

Although trail-building had been nominally completed after 15 years, before the meeting was over, Avery and his allies set the Conference on its next major course, which would dominate the Trail story for more than the next 60 years. They knew the fragility of that first route across the lands of amenable private owners in Maine and across the mid-Atlantic from New York to central Virginia. Even the public lands the path crossed were subject to sudden political decisions to favor a jobs-producing road or highway instead, and old carriage roads were inevitably going to become automobile byways.

OPPOSITE: Screw Augur Falls in the rugged canyon known as Gulf Hagas, a beacon for hikers forever, is now on a short side trail from the A.T. near the southern part of its northernmost 100 miles.

Blazes and Milestones

White blazes painted by volunteer maintainers predominate in marking the way of the Trail, but distance-conscious thru-hikers come up with their own ways of measuring how many miles they have walked from Springer Mountain, Georgia.

CHAPTER 3

Signs, Shelters, and a Whole New Goal

A t that 1937 meeting, the second A.T. era was born—with a series of important consequences for the Trail itself and the role of what became the Appalachian Trail Conservancy.

Edward Ballard, National Park Service (NPS) field coordinator and an Appalachian Mountain Club member, presented to the delegates an Avery-inspired resolution calling for pursuit of "an Appalachian Trailway"—a buffer strip of land through which the Trail and its surroundings would be protected, on private and public lands alike, for those who seek their recreation on foot. It would not be the last time a 30-something ATC official and a mid-level NPS official would team up to try to permanently protect the Trail in an unprecedented way.

While the difference might seem subtle, comparing this new Trailway proposal to the trailway explicitly envisioned by Benton MacKaye in the original ATC constitution and his 1927 speech to the New England Trail Conference illustrates a major conceptual difference between the two leading personalities of the early A.T. project.

MacKaye sought a belt of *protected wilderness*—for various kinds of social betterment—that would be nominally held together by a hiking path. In a 1971 interview with the *AIA Journal*, he bluntly repudiated the Trailway concept as adopted by the Conference and the word itself that he had made prominent at the original 1925 meeting:

> The Appalachian Trail is a wilderness strip; it could be very wide—several miles wide—if possible. It is not a trailway. Actually the trail itself could be a strip no wider than space for a fat man to get through. And that's the trouble: "Trailway" is a very unfortunate word; it gives the impression of a Greyhound bus and a great cement, six-lane highway, which is just the opposite of what the trail is supposed to be. The idea is a foot trail, and if there is a wheel on it at all, there is no point in the Appalachian Trail. People should get that through their heads . . . .

The Avery–Ballard vision adopted by the ATC (and incorporated in all the legislation to come) made the footpath itself preeminent and sought a belt of land to protect the path. "The problems of improving and maintaining [the Trail] alone require constant attention," Ballard said at that June meeting. "Now that the trail is becoming widely known, increased public use actually threatens to bring the closing of some sections which cross public land. The goal of putting through the most feasible route in the shortest possible space of time has been reached, but the continued vigilance of volunteer trail organizations will be needed merely to hold the ground that has been won . . . .

"The challenge now before us is to give the backbone of this skeleton network of trails, the Appalachian Trail, greater strength through improved location and to clothe it with the flesh of enduring life by protective zones of publicly owned land," he said.

Ballard presented a five-point program: designation and preservation of "wild zones" where the Trail crossed wilder public land already; improvement and/or relocation of other parts on public land; "gradual extension of public holdings" by federal and state agencies; acquisition of scenic easements along roads or other public rights-of-way; and development of a chain of shelters "a comfortable day's journey apart." He did not specify how much land would be necessary for this program.

Ballard felt that new legislation would not be necessary, that all that could be accomplished through interstate compacts authorized by the 1936 Park, Parkway, and Recreational-Area Act. The new Congress, after all, was considerably more conservative than the previous two.

"The time has come to face the future and establish the Trail on a permanent and lasting basis," Myron Avery told the crowd. "It may not be something which can be realized immediately, but if it is a sound, definite goal toward which we can aim, we will have pointed the way. That will be sufficient and progress may come as it will. We need more than the bare Trail."

The ATC board was directed to pursue the Ballard plan, and "trailway" became the new byword. Within 14 months, though, it was Mother Nature—rather than Avery's feared "vagaries of changing economic conditions," and another highway, which he brushed off in 1937 as posing "very little interference"—that would determine in major ways the course of the A.T. project for the next decade or more, even before World War II imposed its own challenges.

PREVIOUS SPREAD: Big Bald on the Tennessee–North Carolina border, Cherokee National Forest.
OPPOSITE: Potomac Appalachian Trail Club hikers in 1962 head off the A.T. down toward Nicholson Hollow, where the club still maintains a renovated cabin left over from the time when Shenandoah National Park acquired scores of mountain homesteads.

On September 21, 1938, "The Great Hurricane"—the storms didn't have personal names then—slammed across New England, a Category-5 storm that caught forecasters by surprise and the first major one to hit that region since 1869. Newspaper reports from that time said flooding was the worst in 50 years. Ultimately, more than 600 died because of the storm, including 72 in hardest-hit Massachusetts. The A.T., only 13 months old as a continuous footpath, was broken in many places, the volunteers basically sent back to square one in terms of an open pathway.

Flooding in the mid-Atlantic two years earlier had, to a lesser degree, forced other changes in the Trail route. At Harpers Ferry, West Virginia, for example, where the north-flowing Shenandoah River meets the east-flowing Potomac River along the 19th-century Chesapeake and Ohio Canal, all bridges were destroyed. Until the late 1940s, hikers had to rely on a variety of not-so-reliable ferrymen with flat-bottomed skiffs to get them in and out of town, among them one "Snapper" Roderick, who resembled a turtle when seen in a "cocoon of dirty quilts" in the packing box he called home along the river.

Less than a month after the hurricane, on October 15, 1938, the National Park Service and U.S. Forest Service executed an agreement to promote Ballard's 1937 Trailway concept throughout the route, creating, as an example to others, a protective zone extending *one mile* on either side of the Trail as it passed through national forests and parks.

Under that agreement, neither new parallel roads for motor transportation—such as the divisive Skyline Drive—nor other incompatible development not already authorized would be allowed within the protected zone. Timber cutting would be prohibited within 200 feet of the footpath. The Trail would be relocated where necessary to keep it at least one mile from any undesirable road. A system of campsites, lean-tos, and shelters also was authorized. At the time, about 875 miles of the Trail passed through eight national forests and two national parks.

Beginning with meetings early the following year, all the Trail states except Maine signed similar cooperative Trailway agreements with the National Park Service—the key difference being that the corridor width under these pacts dropped from two miles to a half mile, because of the limited acreage of the state parks and game lands involved.

The pacts formalized the public agencies' recognition of the privately inspired Trail and their commitment to a share of responsibility for its care. While ATC was not a party to these agreements, Avery was involved behind the scenes, and they did serve to institutionalize what had been an active, unique, but informal partnership between the Conference and public agencies—a principal element in the unique nature of the Appalachian Trail project and a keystone of its success to this day.

Notwithstanding the agency-level cooperative agreements, in the mid-1930s Congress had authorized a Blue Ridge Parkway—going as far as Georgia—as an extension of Skyline Drive in central Virginia's Shenandoah Park. Avery, who first thought the Trail and parkway could coexist as parallel routes through southern Virginia, later termed that highway decision "the major catastrophe in Appalachian Trail history." It ultimately displaced nearly 120 miles of the Trail farther to the west in Virginia; no other single external act has displaced so much Trail mileage.

OPPOSITE: The Trail through the thick Maine woods—here near Rangeley—is often described as "rocks and roots." Because the soils are thin and many areas are wet, volunteers use puncheon or bog bridging in some areas to lessen the impact of hikers on the vegetation and reduce erosion.

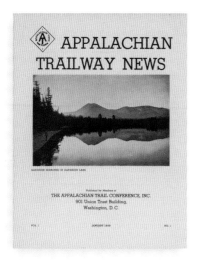

ABOVE: The cover of the January 1939 first edition of the *Appalachian Trailway News*, edited by Jean Stephenson into the 1960s.
OPPOSITE: Also in 1939, Stephenson and other headquarters volunteers weighed everything in their packs to try to get their gear down to 12 pounds for the ATC meeting in Maine.

That relocation was matched in size only by the Maine club's decision in the 1970s and 1980s to replace more than half the original route in that state with trails on ridges rather than roads.

The Trail continued to be broken or damaged by periodic smaller gaps. Some were created by disputes between hikers and landowners. Others were due to the many obstacles to keeping up with Trail work during World War II—from severe weather to lack of hikers and maintainers to increased lumbering to Avery's being called to active duty by the Navy.

Internally after the 1937 meeting, the Conference expanded its capacity for coordinating the Trail/Trailway project and communicating with members and supporters. It improved its guidebooks program and established the *Appalachian Trailway News* as a three-times-a-year magazine in 1939. Dr. Jean Stephenson, the volunteer founding editor, paid the production costs of the first two issues herself and continued as editor until 1964. It became a quarterly in 1972, began five-times-a-year publication in 1976, and continued as the ATC's primary publication—and principal benefit of membership—until June 2005, when it was superseded by the newly named Conservancy's *A.T. Journeys*.

By the late-August 1939 ATC meeting, which took place in the shadow of Katahdin, clubs were reporting the following: major progress in making and erecting signs; barriers to the shelters goal put up by private landowners who liked the Trail but thought shelters would just attract local parties; and a step-by-step restoration of the broken pathway by individual maintainers. The Washington-office volunteers could barely keep up with information requests, and, as the meeting neared, seemed equally worried about keeping their packs under the Avery-suggested limit of 12 pounds (lightweight travel had never gone away as a near-compulsion there, ever since the first "workshop" on it at the founding meeting). Deep in the records are typed lists of what people were taking, with penciled-in notes of what each item weighed on the office postal scale.

Earlier in the month, Walter Greene had written the delegates a "welcome to my beloved state. A long illness, culminating in a serious operation, prevents my being with you," but he recounted the challenges he had faced in 1933 and his pride in mastering them. "If thru this meeting some modest plan evolves for its future maintenance, for the repair of the damage caused by the hurricane, I will be happy. Some day I hope to see again the silver aisle stretching before me."

At the meeting, Avery estimated that, because of the Trailway initiative, "within the next decade, we may expect this protection to have been conferred upon some 1,200 miles of the 2,025-mile route." He hoped the presence of such a large gathering in Maine would bring his home state into the fold, but it didn't. On the other hand, he noted, the 14 shelters built in the last two years (primarily by federal workers) brought the total to 127 along the Trail, and only one state—Maine—was close to having a continuous shelter chain as prescribed by the Ballard proposal and outlined in one of Avery's newer manuals.

For the meeting, the Natural Bridge Appalachian Trail Club of Lynchburg, Virginia, sent in a report that, while 50 percent of its 120 miles would have to be abandoned because of the Blue Ridge Parkway, "the forced change in location is in no way disheartening. What we at once dreaded has turned out to be a big blessing in disguise," abandoning roads for "a spectacular course" to the west.

CONTENTS OF FRAME PACK

	Weight
Gerber frame pack	3 lbs
Clothing	
Wool breeches	1 lb
Flannel shirt	8 oz
Silk shirts x 2...........	8 oz
Handkerchiefs 6	
Silk undies 2	10 oz
Wool undies 2	10 oz
Wool socks 6 x prs	1 lb 3 oz
*Silk socks 4 prs	
Parka	14 oz
*Sweater	6 oz
*Sweat shirt	1 lb 2 oz
Rain suit & hat	1 lb
Bathing suit & cap	12 oz
Tennis slippers	15 oz
Pajamas	9 oz
Toilet articles	7 oz
*Rubbers	15 oz
*Boots	2½ lbs

	Weight
Miscellaneous	
*Guidebook	11 oz (glass - 1 oz)
*First Aid	
*Triangular Bandage	
Bandades	1 Oz
Fly Dope	3 oz
Knife	2 oz
Cup	3 oz
Salt shaker	2 oz
Match case	1 oz
Flashlight	2 oz
Boot grease	3 oz
*Notebook & pencil	
Thread	1 oz

Full pack	14¼ lbs
Underwear	1¼ lbs
All shirts	1 lb 15 oz
Gum and charms	1 oz each

*Not in pack when weighed.

Maine canvas boots	2 lbs 10 oz
Moccasins	1 lb 2 oz
Oxfords	1 lb 10 oz
keds	1 lb 5 oz
1 pr socks wool	4 oz.

Meanwhile during this year, four other "section hikers," all involved in ATC work at some level, reported hiking the whole Trail: Martin and Mary Kilpatrick, Orville Crowder, and George Outerbridge.

Soon, everything would change. At the time of the meeting, Adolf Hitler and Joseph Stalin were concluding their nonaggression pact. There are very few references in ATC files to world events, but during this time government officials such as Avery and Stephenson prefaced brief notes to others with phrases such as, "I just learned that war has broken out in Europe . . ." or "I have been called back to the office because of a war matter . . . ."

Before the end of the year, Avery left the Shipping Board in Washington and moved with his family to New York City as special assistant to the United States attorney, supervising both civil and military litigation involving shipping, since the United States' support for Great Britain and others at that point primarily involved shipping. He nonetheless kept trying to govern the Trail project—remotely and with as frequent trips to the Trail or the Washington offices as he could manage. He remained Conference chairman, and, until early 1941, was also president of the PATC.

The demands of paid work did not stop him from immersing himself in the planning for what would be the last Trail meeting before the United States formally entered the war—in May 1941 at New York's Bear Mountain Inn, where much began in 1922.

Just before the meeting, Major William Welch died at age 72. Arno Cammerer, who had been involved with the Trail from the beginning, too, and had just finished seven years as director of the National Park Service, died that spring as well. The Maine club had lost not only Walter Greene, but also the state forest supervisor and the Civilian Conservation Corps crews on which it depended.

Earle Clapp, acting chief of the Forest Service, delivered a modest warning to the delegates: More hikers were needed to justify continuing federal support for the Trail. Trail use in New England forests "is very encouraging" but "disappointing small" in almost all the southern areas. Despite strong agency support for the A.T. and for hiking in general, "some of our southern men wonder whether the developments so far completed are justified by the use and whether expenditures on additional betterment and construction can be justified. The problem is one of priority."

Clapp urged more efforts toward publicity, especially encouraging hikers to tell their stories, noting a letter he had seen in a magazine from a man who started from Mount Oglethorpe and hiked to Damascus, Virginia: "It was astonishing to me to find so magnificent a trail so little frequented. Outside the limits of the Great Smoky Mountains National Park, I met not a single walker in three weeks of travel."

That, too, would change in time.

Soon after the United States declared war on Japan and then Germany in December 1941, Avery—an officer in the Naval Reserve since 1928—was called to active duty as a lieutenant commander, running a Navy legal office that undertook a fourfold increase in its workload compared to peacetime. He was promoted to commander.

Some parts of the Trail close to military installations were closed to hikers. Maintainers were called off to combat or support roles. Trail maintenance paid the price for those commitments and

new priorities, although shortages of gasoline and tires played no small part in keeping city-based maintainers out of the woods.

The *Appalachian Trailway News* continued without interruption, with hallmark optimism and more of those nostalgic, first-person hiking stories—many from hikers stationed in war zones overseas. One of the war's other effects on the magazine was a steady stream of articles on developments in military gear and food rations that could be adapted for lightweight camping equipment.

With the end of World War II, all Trail-related activities revived with a flourish, although limited appropriations for the park and forest services hampered completion of relocations approved on federal lands, and many years' neglect simply could not be speedily overcome.

However, the Trail's leader was in decline. In late 1946, Avery wrote a friend that he would be "unavailable" for a while. It turned out that he had entered a military hospital for three weeks for treatment of "hypertension"—which he said got worse there, so he checked himself out. He was discharged from the Navy in 1947 as a captain and returned to the admiralty board.

At the same time, the Conference and its partners realized that the cooperative agreements were—and increasingly would be—insufficient to ensure protection of the Trail. In 1945, U.S. Representative Daniel K. Hoch of Pennsylvania, a former member of the ATC board and president of the Blue Mountain Eagle Hiking Club, introduced farsighted legislation to create a national system of foot trails, specifically including the Appalachian Trail. The powerful chairman of the House Committee on Roads pigeonholed that bill. But, the hearings on it were circulated widely by the Conference leadership and served to reinforce the Trailway philosophy and crystallize the movement for its permanent protection. Three years later, Hoch, as a private citizen and board member again, had an amended version of the legislation introduced, but it, too, was pigeonholed.

THE FIRST THRU-HIKER

The bit of Trail history that *was* made that year of 1948 was the appearance of the first "thru-hiker," Earl V. Shaffer of York Springs, Pennsylvania, who reported completing the entire 2,050 miles in an uninterrupted four-month backpacking trip. Shaffer had lost his closest friend while they were in combat in the Pacific Theater and was "walking off the war" by "walking with spring" along the Appalachian Trail he had read about in a magazine.

While he was halfway to Maine, Avery was presiding over the Conference's first postwar regrouping meeting, at Fontana Dam in North Carolina, part of which was devoted to a discussion on how unlikely a thru-hike would be. The chairman was particularly disturbed that Shaffer had no official guidebooks and maps; Shaffer said he wrote for but never received them so instead used oil-company maps and whatever he could pick up at parks and forests along the way.

In July 2011, James McNeely, a West Virginia lawyer and hiker, using Shaffer's diary, photographs, and other records—now in the care of the Smithsonian Museum of American History—challenged the account of the iconic Shaffer, who died in 2002. While trying to retrace his steps and microanalyzing his journal versus his book, but also making several assumptions about Shaffer's state of mind and decision-making that only Shaffer himself could rebut, McNeely alleged that "The Crazy One" had skipped 10 percent or more of the route as he did, indeed, walk from Georgia to Maine. Shaffer's account is still accepted as the first reported thru-hike; the ATC neither investigates nor endorses such reports.

"Now the one thing about the whole trek that caused the most comment—my traveling alone . . . . For my part, I preferred it so. Before the war, there were two of us who trailed together, and we had our dreams, as many others have had, of hiking the Appalachian Trail some day. But, Iwo Jima was the end of life's trail for him, leaving me to travel alone. From him, I learned most of my woodcraft and my abiding love of all outdoors. Walter Winemiller was a pardner such as one may have only once in life, and no incentive could have been stronger to carry me over the long high Trail than remembering we always wanted to hike it together."

—EARL V. SHAFFER, 1949, *Appalachian Trailway News*

After he reported his feat to the ATC, Shaffer underwent at least one "grilling," as he would later put it, primarily by Stephenson—place questions, people questions, photographic evidence, Trail-condition questions—before she and, through her, Avery would accept the report. Stephenson did note two "off track" sections, which Shaffer acknowledged and blamed on poor signage or unmarked relocations during that recovery period.

Shaffer hiked the Trail again in 1965, from the other direction, and once more as a 50th-anniversary trek in 1998 at age 79—complaining bitterly all the way about route changes from roads up to mountaintops away from towns. Although he had stayed away from Trail functions after a dispute with NPS land-acquisition workers in the 1980s, he resumed his involvement in the mid-1990s with standing-room-only shows of his slides (accompanied by his poems and songs) until his final, extended illness hospitalized him in 2001.

OPPOSITE: Earl V. Shaffer atop Baxter Peak of Katahdin in August 1948, just before he became the first to report an end-to-end, single-journey hike of the Appalachian Trail, documented by his slides and notes.

He was named president of the York Hiking Club after his first hike and, once he had satisfied Avery and Stephenson, was appointed ATC corresponding secretary, providing advice to would-be hikers of all kinds and taking a burden off the Washington volunteers.

Shaffer's hike drew at least two lines across the story of the Appalachian Trail. Although then, as now, more than 99.9 percent of the users of the Trail are day hikers and groups of two or four for a weekend or week—or club members out for an overnight—the notion was forever gone that a single backpacker could not walk that whole distance in a continuous hike.

The second break in pattern reflected that human recreational achievement. Shaffer garnered publicity throughout the country's major news outlets and then a full-length article in *National Geographic* about him and the Trail. From then on, local and national publicity about the Trail shifted markedly from the achievements of the "recreational maintainer" to those of recreational thru-hikers, although their numbers would not be significant for another quarter century. Two more complete section-hikes and two more thru-hikes—by Eugene M. Espy of Georgia and Chester F. Dziengielewski of Connecticut, walking in different directions—were the next reported, in 1951.

"The mountain people I met along the Trail were kind, hospitable, and interesting. Many who took me in for the night were poor, but they willingly shared what they had . . . . My faith in mankind was renewed. Reading the Bible, meditating, and enjoying God in nature made my hike an uplifting religious experience."

—EUGENE ESPY, 1951

THE END OF THE AVERY ERA

In 1951, Avery could once again pronounce the Trail a continuous footpath—hurricane and a decade of other storm damage repaired, the shift from east to west across southern Virginia done, and a glorious new route in northeast Tennessee across the 6,000-foot Roan Highlands, alive with acres of Catawba rhododendron and less flashly but much more rare flora.

The last relocation necessitated by Blue Ridge Parkway construction was opened on The Priest, a mountain on the Religious Range in the Pedlar ranger district of the George Washington National Forest in Virginia. Avery planned an elaborate ceremony that was ultimately cancelled by heavy rain and fog and members' schedule conflicts. His prepared remarks, perhaps the most eloquent of his later years, publicly articulated another principal element in the unique nature of the Appalachian Trail project: the pivotal role of the volunteer.

The Trail until then had been associated most often with the founders and leaders of various organizations. However, Avery's text argued:

This Trail might well, instead of "Appalachian Trail," have been termed, "The Anonymous Trail," in recognition of the fact that many, many people . . . have labored on [it]. They have asked for no return nor recognition nor reward. They have contributed to the project simply by reasons of the pleasure found in trail-making and in the realization that they were, perhaps, creating something which would be a distinct contribution to the American recreational system and the training of American people.

In this period, many of the forest and park districts and their allied volunteers in clubs north and south of the major Virginia–Tennessee relocations were concentrating anew on completing the system of open overnight shelters envisioned by the Ballard proposal and Trailway movement of the late 1930s.

Late in 1951, Avery announced that he would not be a candidate for reelection as chairman the following June at the 12th ATC conference—again at Skyland, Virginia—where he had first taken over from G. Arthur Perkins and later faced down the "revolt" over Skyline Drive. What was not widely known within the Trail community was that he had had at least one heart attack and was simultaneously with this announcement being forced to retire on disability from the admiralty board.

Beginning early in 1952, Avery was hospitalized for months with what Stephenson called an intestinal ailment, as she and others undertook all the meeting preparations he normally would have dictated. Yet, he was not totally removed—his files from just one week that March are more than an inch thick with letters and memoranda he dictated (apparently from a hospital bed), about the meeting and other matters. About a week before the Skyland session opened, he "authorized and directed" his senior vice chairman to preside in his absence.

In his written final report, after noting that the Conference was sound financially and all programs were on track, Avery stated, "The Appalachian Trail derives much of its strength and appeal from its uninterrupted and practically endless character. This is an attribute which must be preserved. I view the existence of this pathway and the opportunity to travel it, day after day without interruption, as a distinct aspect of our American life."

He outlined a number of clear threats to maintaining a continuous route "immune from invasion and development"—setting the stage for more than 30 years of congressional and federal administrative activity ahead. He continued:

> The problem lies in the connecting units of privately owned land [between publicly owned areas], much of which will soon become subject to intense development. Protest against federal or state domination is, of course, a popular theme these days. However, the unexpected penetration and development of areas in private ownership . . . will serve to fortify our conclusion that some form of public protection must be extended to the Trail system if it is to survive as a through, continuous recreational unit. The problem is very real. Its solution and an ability to make effective that desired solution present to our successors an issue and labor in comparison with which the efforts of the past two decades are indeed minute.

ABOVE: Eugene Espy of Georgia along a road in Maine en route to becoming the second person to report a complete thru-hike of the A.T.

Development and increase of population may . . . possibly produce the unavoidable result that, in lieu of a continuous uninterrupted Trail, we shall have to content ourselves with disconnected segments of an extensive length. We enter now in Appalachian Trail history the stage where emphasis and attention must be focused on the benefits resulting from this opportunity to travel the forests of the eastern United States, as our forefathers knew them. While this theme is far from pleasant, I would be remiss, indeed, if I failed to note the inevitable extraordinarily rapid change to be anticipated in the character of the private lands through which the Trail route passes . . . .

A trail and its markings do not constitute any intrusion upon naturalness of the forest wilderness. Trails should be marked and maintained in a manner to eliminate the necessity of labor and uncertainty in finding one's route. They should be an open course, a joy for travel. In that manner, without concern for route finding, the traveller will derive full benefit from his surroundings. This is what we have sought to accomplish in our constant and unending emphasis on the indicated standards of Appalachian Trail marking and maintenance.

Elected to succeed Avery was his senior vice chairman, Murray H. Stevens of New York, former chairman of the New York–New Jersey Trail Conference and another of the original pioneers. He had been actively involved in both the organization work and on-the-ground trail-building and upkeep since 1928. By 1930, he had built the 55-mile New York section east of the Hudson River that would link up with the Connecticut section built in 1930–33 by Ned Anderson.

Avery, named honorary chairman at the meeting in tribute to his long service to the Trail project, died just eight weeks later, four months shy of his 53rd birthday. The philosophical MacKaye, 20 years Avery's elder, would outlive him by 23 years.

Avery was later said to be ill for a year from what the *Appalachian Trailway News* termed "the 'nerve fatigue' from the intensive demands of his Navy work"—working himself to death. Trying to ease up from 25 years of intensive occupational and avocational drive, the ATC's "skipper" collapsed and died on a grassy hummock atop the old fortifications of Fort Anne National Historic Park in Nova Scotia while on a trip with his son, Hal, to research family history. A doctor who rushed to Avery from across the street told Hal the final heart attack was so massive that his father probably died before he hit the ground. A small part of Avery's legacy was an extensive memo to the ATC board and core volunteers on what needed to be done after he left office.

Shelters

Most modern overnight shelters and accompanying privies are the work of volunteer Trail maintainers in local clubs, but some remain from the 1930s work of government partners. In the White Mountains, a chain of enclosed, staffed Appalachian Mountain Club huts provides a different experience.

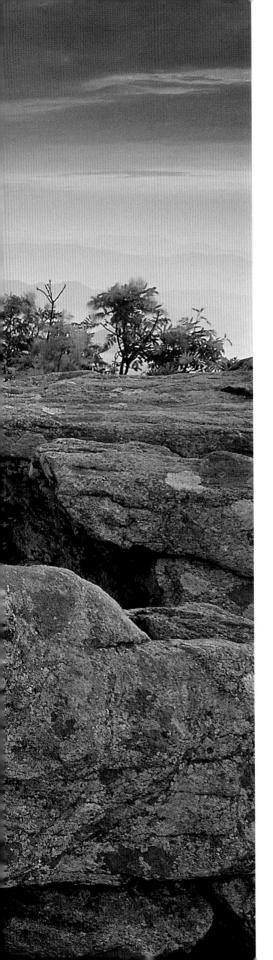

CHAPTER 4

Regathering the Momentum, Gaining the Prize

J ust as strongly as Avery had labored against the odds to make MacKaye's wilderness-belt concept a practical hiking reality—leading a widely separated collection of probably no more than 250 volunteers, total—his successors in the next four decades would labor to fulfill Avery's own concept of a secure, protective Trailway. At the same time, they, too, had to struggle with relocations, maintenance, completion of the lean-to chain, and landowner/hiker relationships.

Chairman Murray H. Stevens—a Princeton-educated engineer four years Avery's senior who had led the routing of the Trail between Connecticut and the Hudson River in the 1920s and '30s—worked on ATC business from New York, frequently traveling to Washington, D.C., and elsewhere for meetings. Much of the day-to-day work of guiding the Trail project was carried on by a small handful of dedicated volunteers in Washington.

Foremost among them was Dr. Jean Stephenson, a long-term Avery associate and Navy Department employee who was a lawyer and genealogist as well as a professional editor. She edited and published the *Appalachian*

Trailway News, guidebooks, and other publications; organized Conference meetings; served as liaison to federal and state officials and clubs; provided background to the officers on an array of issues; and also cleared Trail in Maine. (In her late 70s, after Florence Nichol had become *ATN* editor, Stephenson was still editing A.T. guidebooks—even from hospital beds.)

Among those people who were organizing Washington volunteers nightly at the Potomac Appalachian Trail Club headquarters to answer mail and A.T. guidebook orders was Fred Blackburn, Conference secretary, whose wife, Ruth, became PATC president in the early 1960s and ATC chair in the early 1980s. Another stalwart was Sadye Giller, the treasurer, who spent nearly every Saturday afternoon at the ATC headquarters for 22 years, keeping the financial records.

Whether significant use of the Trail was rebounding to levels the Forest Service could again use to justify its investment is not clear in the project's records, but a little bit of hiker history was made in 1952—to be basically overlooked, or reworked, ever since. On April 26, Mildred Norman, 44, set off with a Philadelphia friend, Richard Lamb, from Mount Oglethorpe heading north to Katahdin. According to Marta Daniels's 2005 biography, the pair finished in October, but the terse postcards they periodically sent to the ATC (signed "Richard Lamb and Mildred," from which many inferred Mr. and Mrs.) showed they did not follow the Shaffer/Espy pattern—instead skipping to New England from Pennsylvania and then going "backwards," with a hike of the Long Trail squeezed in.

The following New Year's Day, Norman renamed herself "Peace Pilgrim"—more than 20 years before Trail names came into vogue on the A.T.—and started a 5,000-mile walk for peace from California to New York, the beginning of her three-decade crusade. This was at the height of the McCarthy era. Because she did not hike alone and did not walk strictly from one terminus to the other without deviation, Mildred Norman has seldom been accepted as the first woman A.T. thru-hiker.

That title has almost always been awarded to someone with just the set of unusual attributes and eccentricities to draw the national news media like bears to honey: Emma Rowena Gatewood of Gallipolis, Ohio. Farm-tending mother of 11 and grandmother of 23, she was 67 when she first hiked the whole A.T. in 1955, from south to north. (She had failed miserably the year before, barely making it out of Maine's Baxter State Park.) She had read the 1949 *National Geographic* article about Earl Shaffer and decided to try a thru-hike herself.

The hike itself would have been enough for headlines, but she famously walked in high-top Keds with a homemade denim sling sack, a cotton blanket, a raincoat, and a plastic shower curtain for shelter, altogether never more than 17 pounds. Although the A.T.'s core volunteers had been competing among themselves for 25 years to keep weights under 12 or 13 pounds, she was pronounced an ultralight pioneer. All that and more—seldom cooking, relying heavily on strangers' kindnesses, hiking frequent 20-mile days—brought in *Sports Illustrated* and, ultimately, the still-new *Today* show: serious publicity for the Trail. Despite complaining that it was not the "lark" she thought it would be, she completed another thru-hike two years later and did the whole Trail again in sections by the mid-1960s.

PREVIOUS SPREAD: Dawn at Jane Bald, North Carolina–Tennessee border. ABOVE: Emma "Grandma" Gatewood of Ohio, the first woman to report a thru-hike in the same continuous direction, inspired thousands for her grit, simple gear, and candor. She was 67 years old on her first of three successful hikes.

When writing her obituary in 1973, Edward B. Garvey, a longtime volunteer and himself an inspiration for thousands—he wrote books about thru-hiking in the 1970s—recalled that when he first hiked in 1970, "Her name and her exploits were mentioned to me more times than those of all previous hikers combined. There was something about this little old lady doggedly pursuing her goal in good weather and bad that seemed to make an everlasting imprint in the minds of those she met and visited with."

In 1957, although they were not together, "Grandma" Gatewood was joined in reporting a thru-hike by more publicity-adverse Dorothy Laker, who likewise went on to walk the whole Trail twice more, hiking for a week through northeast Tennessee with Earl Shaffer on her second trek.

In 1955 and 1957, they were the only two reported thru-hikers—the only time that the registry was all women. In Mildred Norman's year, she made it 33 percent women. In the stretch from Avery's 1936 accomplishment to the end of the 1950s, only four women were among the 21 people reporting "end-to-end" hikes of the A.T.—19 percent, a trend that stuck throughout the 20th century, although as of this writing the cumulative percentage of women 2,000-Milers has slightly exceeded 25 percent.

"Hiking promotes relaxation and peace of mind. It gets me away from the trivialities of the workaday world. It sets up a storehouse of pleasant memories for the rocking-chair age of 80. It provides a time for thinking and dreaming. It makes me very rich in new possessions—the mountains I crossed become mine, as do the shelters I stay at, and, even though I am an absentee landlord, they are all still in my domain . . . . Even though I had always lived in a city, I suspected that the forests were my natural country. My hikes confirmed this feeling. I found education, inspiration, relaxation, and contentment."

—DOROTHY LAKER, 1957, 1964, 1962–1972

IMPROVEMENT BY RELOCATIONS

The 1950s and 1960s saw many significant, voluntary relocations of the Trail—some of them 75 to 150 miles long and requiring two or more years of steady work, most notably those that had begun in the 1940s in the South between Roanoke and the Smokies. Beyond the need to get away from more than half of the Blue Ridge Parkway (while weaving around the other half), the changes sought to refine and enhance the route and add peaks, views, southern balds, and safer stream crossings.

In 1958, the Conference accepted the recommendation of the Georgia Appalachian Trail Club and moved the southern terminus of the Trail north 20 miles to its present point at Springer Mountain. The area around Mount Oglethorpe, originally chosen as part of a relationship with

THE APPALACHIAN TRAIL

the developer of the Tate Estates, had become too commercially developed to be compatible with the A.T. concept.

The spreading developments driven by the post-World War II economic boom were affecting all regions of the Trail to some degree. The interstate highway system—a monster version of "townless highways" MacKaye himself had proposed decades earlier for Massachusetts—was authorized in the middle of the decade after years of automobile-industry pressure. In his parting message as chairman, Murray Stevens wrote, "I consider the only solution for the permanence of the Appalachian Trail as a 'wilderness footpath' is in public ownership. The ever-increasing population and constant expansions of the seaboard, with resultant growth in rural living and development, leaves no alternative. I would propose a 'green belt' of public lands with the Trail acting as a spinal cord linking them together."

"There is a feeling of always being surrounded by all the good things, like love and peace and joy. It seems like a protective surrounding, and there is an unshakeableness within, which takes you through any situations you need to face."

—MILDRED NORMAN, first woman to hike the Appalachian Trail in a single year, 1952

In 1961, the Conference elected as its chairman another Maine native—Stanley A. Murray, then living in Kingsport, Tennessee, and one force behind the Trail's relocation to the Roan Highlands. He would hold the position for 14 years, a tenure second only to Avery's. (A constitutional change in 1972 limited the tenure of each elected office to six consecutive years.)

It was during this period that the goal of securing a permanently protected Trailway on public lands was fully adopted and initially implemented. The work that began in the mid-1930s—as the footpath itself was finally becoming a continuous reality—was about to close its penultimate era.

Real threats to the Trail compelled this step, as Avery had foreseen. Commercial development had already led to the abandonment of Mount Oglethorpe and the Amicalola Range, the tail of the Blue Ridge. Congress was again considering major new parkways in Georgia and New Jersey that would have pushed the Trail aside, but reconsidered after major grassroots protests by Conference and maintaining-club members.

Ski resorts, mountaintop second-home developments, a highway-building trend, communications towers, mining and timber cutting, various proposals for more skyline drives for an increasingly (auto)mobile America, and the inevitable advance of the East Coast megalopolis had an enormous cumulative effect on the Trail environment. MacKaye's somewhat prematurely envisioned threat of four decades before was becoming more real.

OPPOSITE: Tennessee Eastman Hiking Club volunteers at a safety talk before working on a major 1952 relocation south of the Virginia line.

To meet the constant onslaught of development, the ATC sought federal legislation again. Meeting in the lamplight at Chairback Mountain Camps in Maine in August 1963, Chairman Murray, Jean Stephenson, Sadye Giller, and Sidney Tappen from Massachusetts agreed it was time to resurrect the legislative work begun in the 1940s by Representative Daniel Hoch.

As it turned out, Congress was considering the formation of the Land and Water Conservation Fund for the Interior Department, through which funds for the Trail project would be funneled 15 years later. It was also working on the Wilderness Act, and Benton MacKaye lent his support to the related efforts. The climate seemed better than in the austere war and early postwar years.

Murray called a meeting of ATC officers and other interested parties that fall in Washington. At a later social gathering, a supporter from Wisconsin mentioned the problems to the senator from his home state, Gaylord Nelson, whose committee assignments and personal inclinations made him an ideal standard-bearer. Within a few weeks, Senator Nelson indicated his willingness to help.

"The Appalachian Trail is not a stunt in heroics or of endurance . . . . It is rather an opportunity for someone to find himself as a creature in nature. It is a way of life and an experience in living."

—WALTER BOARDMAN, section-hiker, 1960, chaired ATC legislative committee

In May 1964, he introduced legislation that would have declared the Trail and sufficient lands on either side to be "in the public interest" and a resource requiring preservation. That bill did not advance in that election year, with its early congressional recess, but, reintroduced in 1965, it received vigorous support in Senate hearings.

At the same time, President Lyndon B. Johnson directed Secretary of the Interior Stewart Udall to develop recommendations for a national system of trails that would "copy the great Appalachian Trail in all parts of America," as he put it in his February 8, 1965, message to Congress on "Natural Beauty." Records in the Lyndon B. Johnson Library indicate that that idea originated in the office of the First Lady and through the work of Nash Castro, assistant director and later director of the National Park Service's National Capital Region and her liaison to the Interior Department. (Lady Bird Johnson herself told her staff near the end of her husband's presidency that one of the things she wanted to do after they left Washington was to hike the Appalachian Trail.)

The Interior Department's Bureau of Outdoor Recreation, which had completed such a project two years earlier (gaining little lasting positive attention), began a new study. By fall, several members of Congress were already introducing bills to establish such a trails system. Most of the proposals had deficiencies regarding the Appalachian Trail.

OPPOSITE: The A.T. looping along the northern Presidential Range (in the distance) inspires a hiker on the Gulfside Trail, which roughly parallels it from a point where the two trails join just north of Mount Washington, the highest peak of New England, in New Hampshire's White Mountain National Forest.

The Conference pulled together a legislative committee chaired by Dr. Walter S. Boardman, a retired Long Island schools superintendent who had finished hiking the whole Trail in 1960 and had been on the board of The Nature Conservancy. He would write later, "[The ATC] was the first conservation organization that I joined, and it has always been something very special. The Trail itself has profoundly affected my life . . . . It was the visual evidence of the destruction of nature that turned me into the conservation effort." His committee worked with the bureau to draft more acceptable legislation, later proposed by the administration itself and introduced by Senator Henry Jackson and Representative Roy Taylor, the chairmen of the authorizing committees in the Senate and House.

After extensive hearings in 1967, in the middle of the socially and politically tumultuous year of 1968—a year of assassinations and increasingly violent protests against the Vietnam War—the Senate passed the proposed National Trails System Act, the House approved a variation, and House–Senate conferees resolved the differences. On October 2, 1968, President Johnson signed Public Law 90-543, along with seven other pieces of legislation, including the Wild and Scenic Rivers Act. That was and is a signature day in the history of the Appalachian Trail. On Lady Bird Johnson's calendar for the day: "Signing ceremony for Redwoods National Park."

That key statute in Conference history provided for a national system of trails. It specifically designated two. It designated the Appalachian Trail as the first "national scenic trail"—first alphabetically and because it was the only completed, marked trail of those under consideration. The Pacific Crest Trail (PCT), to run through California, Oregon, and Washington, was also designated. The PCT idea had been in the works for decades; it would allow equestrians, while the A.T. would be limited to hikers.

The National Park Service, through the secretary of the interior, was given principal administrative responsibility for the newly named Appalachian National Scenic Trail, in consultation with the U.S. Forest Service, through the secretary of agriculture. (The roles of the agencies were reversed for the Pacific Crest Trail.)

"My A.T. hike is, without question, the most formidable experience of my life, and I know, from [a] brief encounter with Ed Garvey, that I could only have had this experience because of a few caring, persistent, and loving individuals."

—CAROLYN EBEL, 1995–1997

The law directed the Interior Department to establish the permanent route and publish it with maps and descriptions in the *Federal Register*, the official daily journal of the federal government. That publication triggered a provision giving states and localities along the Trail two years in which to acquire privately owned corridor lands in their jurisdictions.

After that two-year period, the park service was authorized to take whatever action was necessary to preserve and protect the Trail—through cooperative agreements, scenic and other protective easements, land acquisitions and exchanges, or accepting land donations. As a last resort, if negotiations failed, it could condemn the needed land under the principle of eminent domain. If condemnation were used, the act stated, a corridor of up to 25 acres, or 200 feet, per mile could be acquired. A sum of $5 million was authorized for land-acquisition appropriations—or more than $31 million in today's dollars. At the time, about 1,032 miles—roughly half the Trail—was located on either private lands or on roads, some of which were newly paved and becoming heavily used.

One of the most significant other provisions of the act for the Conference, beyond the authorizations to acquire the land for the public, was Section 7(h), which authorized formal agreements between the Interior Department and nonfederal entities to "operate, develop, and maintain" the A.T.

OPPOSITE: One of the many fords required of rivers in the northern 100 miles of the A.T. in Maine.

Weather

Rain and snow, as well as sunny days and summer heat, shape the hiker's experience of the Trail just as they have shaped the Appalachian environment for eons.

CHAPTER 5

Sea Changes for the Trail and Its Steward

The passage of the act marked the midpoint of the first significant period of growth for the Conference itself. Individual memberships—attracted by the battle to protect the Trail and a 1967 *Reader's Digest* article—grew from 600 early in Stan Murray's tenure to approximately 10,000 by 1975.

The meetings commitment of the board of managers likewise grew from 30 minutes after general Conference meetings every three years to two weekend-long meetings per year. Board committees implemented new programs and assisted with the volunteer workload.

Passage of the act made it evident to the board that the Conference could operate no longer solely as an organization of volunteers, no matter how dedicated and efficient they were. A third era for the organization was beginning to form. The ATC, for starters, would need an accountable presence in Washington, D.C., to coordinate work with the National Park Service and Forest Service representatives and to reinforce the overworked office volunteers.

Colonel Lester L. Holmes, about to retire from the Army and an A.T. hiker by virtue of many years as a Scoutmaster, had been the ATC's volunteer slide custodian since 1966 and was then drafted into service "hauling bags of mail to the post office" as information requests surged. In October 1968, he was hired as part-time "administrative officer," the ATC's first paid position. One of the first things he did was help produce a 28-minute "motion picture to help tell the story about the 'longest continuously marked trail in the world.'" A year later, his job was expanded to full-time "executive secretary," a title changed two months later to "executive director."

Gradually, as budget adjustments could be made, additional staff members were hired to handle the Conference's day-to-day operations while volunteers continued to maintain the Trail and to set policy through the board and its committees.

"You can get 20 minutes from home, and it's a whole other world." —CHRISTINA M. FERRARA-FRITH, 1987, *The New York Times*

THE PROBLEM OF OVERUSE

Growth in Conference membership and activities went hand in hand with an increase in hiking and backpacking throughout the country. This increase was sparked not only by the ATC's higher public profile during the battle for the trails act, but also by the advent of manufactured lightweight backpacking equipment and a business-model shift for major chain outfitters away from climbing to less technical recreation; such new periodicals as *Backpacker* magazine; publication of the Interior Department's *Trails for America*; and a resurgence of appreciation by young people of nature and the outdoors.

While the 1960s had seen the Conference concentrating on protecting the Trail from incompatible or adverse outside development, the major threat in the first half of the 1970s seemed to come from Trail users—or, more precisely, overusers. This was a serious problem along much of the footpath, which had not been located, designed, or constructed with the thought of so many boots hitting the erosion-prone tread of the mountain ridges so often.

In 1969, for example, only 10 more names were added to the roster of 2,000-Milers, and the average number of end-to-end hikes reported per year since 1948 was two—including six years with no reports. In just the next five years, 234 more hikes were posted to the registry.

It is not that thru-hiker use (an average 156 days of walking) is overuse, but the growth in long-distance hiking was a sign of growth in the Trail's popularity—unscientific statistics, but the only ones available, then and now. (Thru-hikers, despite the attention given them for their accomplishments, account for no more than one half of one percent of Trail users, the bulk of which are day hikers or buddy groups of two or four out for a weekend or a week of backpacking.)

During the hearings on the legislation, club and local agency officials produced an estimate that three to four million persons a year visited the Trail, an estimate that was held on to until the turn of the century. One university survey then produced a new look that was extrapolated to

PREVIOUS SPREAD: Stream on the slopes of Mount Moosilauke, New Hampshire.
OPPOSITE: Bog bridging near Poplar Ridge Lean-to in Maine, north of Saddleback Mountain, protects the wetlands from hikers' impact.

3.3 million. Another survey a few years later, also underwritten by the National Park Service but employing many more on-the-Trail surveyors, put the number at two million.

Benton MacKaye, then 92 and long since retired and back in Shirley Center, Massachusetts, had something to say at the time about use of the Trail. When Earl Shaffer's hike was first publicized, MacKaye had called such treks "stunts," although he did welcome the young Pennsylvanian into his home (while Shaffer never met Myron Avery face-to-face). Asked on the 50th anniversary of publication of his 1921 article what he considered to be the purpose of the Trail, he replied:

> The ultimate purpose? There are three things: (1) to walk; (2) to see; (3) to see what you see. I had to wait about 35 years for the first real response to my article—a long time! Then, an important book was written in 1967 called *The Appalachian Trail: Wilderness on the Doorstep*, by Ann and Myron Sutton. They took their time; they did not rush; they saw what they saw. They did not make the trail a race course or a race track. Some people like to record how speedily they can traverse the length of the trail, but I would give a prize for the ones who took the longest time.

During this period, Conference resources were rechanneled into informational and educational programs aimed at hikers, backpackers, and neighboring landowners—to develop a "Trail ethic" that would help alleviate damage to the natural surroundings. "The conference had always been hiker-service-oriented—service to the hiker at the lowest cost," Lester Holmes recalled toward the end of the 1970s. "Our publications were quite good, but, with this new emphasis, the demand for guidebooks grew, and the need for more frequent updating was necessary."

The gasoline-supply crises of the mid-1970s helped to moderate the year-to-year increases in Trail use, giving maintainers and educators a chance to catch up. It also gave Trail maintainers and their staff support time to devise—a lot of engineers in this group!—new ways to construct treadway and design routes that would better handle traffic that otherwise would have destroyed the land.

Still, in places heavy Trail use had damaged "neighbor relations" along the footpath, and lands were being closed off. Commercial developers were aggressively seeking neighboring farms and forests in the inflationary, speculative land-buying spirit of the decade, too. The Trail was forced back onto roads in many places.

THE RESULTS OF THE NATIONAL TRAILS SYSTEM ACT

Meanwhile, both the Conference and the Potomac Appalachian Trail Club, its landlord in a shared Washington townhouse, were growing in membership, activities, and responsibilities. More space was needed, so, in August 1972, the Conference moved up the Potomac River to Harpers Ferry, West Virginia, about a mile and a half from the Trail at that time but only three blocks from the post office where hikers collected resupply boxes. The small staff worked out of the Brackett House, a government-owned building on Camp Hill in Harpers Ferry National Historical Park that today serves as the park's headquarters.

ABOVE: Lester Holmes, first ATC executive director, points up the Potomac River on a visit with then-U.S. Representative Goodloe E. Byron of Maryland—ironically in the direction of the pedestrian bridge into Harpers Ferry, West Virginia, that would be built and named for Byron after his untimely death.

Less than two years after the 1968 act's passage, the two lead federal agencies took the first public steps to implement it with new cooperative agreements between or among the National Park Service, U.S. Forest Service, and the Appalachian Trail Conference. Agreements between the NPS and 10 of the 14 Trail states, encouraging them to acquire and manage corridor lands outside federal park and forest areas, were signed between 1971 and 1975.

Behind the scenes, everyone needed to know officially where the Trail was at that time. Volunteers and agency workers were drafted to lay down large white panels along the entire route for photography flyovers at 9,000 feet above the terrain. Then, they were called back in to confirm the photographs were correct and label major peaks and other landmarks.

The preliminary "official" A.T. route with 86 pages of maps from the flyovers was published in February 1971 and approved in final form that October, triggering the two-year period of state and local preference in the acquisition process called for by the National Trails System Act.

BELOW: Volunteers coordinated by Holmes place white flags along the Trail for a flyover photography project that produced the first official route for the A.T. as a national scenic trail.

Big Rock　Big Butt　Ball Ground　Unaka Mtn　Green Ridge Knob　No Business Knob　Roan Mtn　Flattop　Flint Ridge　Little Bald　Big Bald　Sugarloaf

Jones Meadow

S-218

ABOVE: During the contentious early routing of the Trail across North Carolina, Japanese-American photographer George Masa produced and labeled panoramic images of the ranges, such as this one from Camp Creek Bald, that helped guide decisions.

BELOW: A rare snapsnot of George Masa with Myron Avery.

The Forest Service, with hundreds of miles of Trail through eight national forests, concentrated its acquisition program on private tracts for the A.T. within the forest boundaries in those early years of the protection program. It acquired large tracts whenever possible, rather than just a linear corridor. It would be January 1979—with a property in New York—before the Interior Department purchased a single easement or a single acre for the Appalachian Trail corridor outside the boundaries of other units of the park system.

Despite the assurances of the 1968 act, some Conference members at the time were concerned that the relatively narrow statutory corridor would not give sufficient protection to the broader Trail environment and that what remained of a "wilderness" character would be lost.

Chairman Stan Murray, spurred by those concerns, launched in 1971–72 an intensive search for a feasible solution. He proposed a relatively broad corridor along the Trail in which the character of the land and the lifestyles of its residents would be preserved. In November 1972, the board of managers resolved "to seek the establishment of an Appalachian Greenway encompassing the Appalachian Trail and of sufficient width to provide a nationally significant zone for dispersed types of recreation, wildlife habitat, scientific study, and timber and watershed management, as well as to provide vicarious benefits to the American people."

That greenway concept envisioned a primitive or wilderness zone acquired by purchases or easements and embracing the footpath, with a surrounding rural or countryside zone of up to 10 miles out from the primitive zone. The countryside zone would consist of largely private property preserved through land-use planning. The ATC went so far as to trademark the term "Appalachian Greenway," soon after it trademarked the classic A.T. diamond as a Trail marker.

The Conference set up a task force, contracted for a feasibility study, and would breathe new life into the dormant Appalachian Highlands Association by electing its own directors as the AHA board and giving it affiliate status.

The consultant's study was accepted by the board in November 1974 and given special attention in June 1975, when a record-high 1,100 persons or more marked the Conference's meeting at Boone, North Carolina, in its golden-anniversary year as an organization. However, other issues soon superseded it for the principal focus of the Conference, among them a concern over lack of National Park Service progress in acquiring lands for the already legislated corridor.

At the Boone meeting, Stan Murray stepped down as chairman, and M. Zoebelein of New York City was elected to succeed him. The new chairman, an accountant involved in several local organizations, would emphasize fiscal management and other organizational matters—"getting our house in order"—as membership continued to grow and the need for long-range planning became clear.

Holmes, who in 1970 had become the Conference's first life member, soon retired as executive director, but he remained active in the archives and reporting relocations until his death in 1984. (He found 254 unreported relocations right after retirement while updating for the U.S. Geological Survey all Trail-related quadrangle maps, which were 25 years old.) Paul C. Pritchard, a political-policy professional from Georgia, was recruited to succeed him in 1975.

THE FIRST APPALACHIAN TRAIL BEST SELLER

Out on the Trail, perhaps first among that surge of thru-hikers to come was Ed Garvey, recently retired chief financial officer of the National Science Foundation and lifelong hiker, setting out from Springer Mountain—not only to hike but to take notes on Trail and shelter conditions (and, as it turned out, litter and other trash). Although all that produced reams of data—indeed, it led to the consistently best-selling annual *Appalachian Trail Data Book* as a hiking essential—the real gift emerged from his joy. As thru-hiker and author Larry Luxenberg later wrote, Garvey belied the typical "ascetic and stoic," give-me-space thru-hiker. "He's one of the most gregarious people ever to hike the A.T. During his 1970 thru-hike, people continually met him with food, drink, and various festivities. Garvey's hike was less of a lone adventure than a roving party," wrote Luxenberg.

At a time when such books could be counted on one hand, Garvey's *Appalachian Hiker: Adventure of a Lifetime* became the best-selling book about the Trail of all time—until Bill Bryson's *A Walk in the Woods* surpassed it tenfold in the late 1990s. "[It] was a landmark in the popularization of backpacking in general and the Appalachian Trail in particular. Nothing matched it in popular impact" until 1998, veteran maintainer Maurice Forrester wrote after Garvey's death in September 1999. "What has been less frequently noted is that Ed's hike also served to galvanize the Appalachian Trail cadre of volunteer Trail maintainers. These anonymous stalwarts of the Trail came to realize—because of Ed—how critically important they were in the scheme of things." Like Shaffer before him, Garvey was soon ATC corresponding secretary and an active board member.

BELOW: In the 1970s, the thru-hike memoirs of club and ATC leader Ed Garvey triggered the first major wave of long-distance backpackers to hit the Trail.

MACKAYE'S DEATH AND A NEW HOME FOR THE ATC

Near the end of 1975, on December 11, Benton MacKaye, who had been blind for a number of years, died in his sleep at Shirley Center, Massachusetts, three months short of his 97th birthday. On June 10, 1978, following two years of negotiations with a niece and MacKaye's literary executor, Lester Holmes "scattered Benton's ashes in the meadow behind the cottage as he had requested."

In 1976, the Conference moved its headquarters a few blocks around Camp Hill to its present location, once a three-story building reduced to two floors after a dynamite-truck explosion miles away broke its windows in 1948 and the absentee landlord failed to protect the top floor against damage from the elements. The structure the ATC bought was built in 1892 by Potomac Council No. 16 of the Sons of Jonadab, a men's temperance group offering an alternative to Harpers Ferry's 13 saloons of the day. In 1976, it served as the meeting place for the 32-man Harpers Ferry Cooking Club.

Over the years, the building had also housed Pop Trinkle's soda counter, the local opera house, a combination gas station and automobile sales and service agency, an Interwoven Sock Company mill, apartments, a gift shop, and a private residence. The first property bought by the Conference, its mortgage was retired on time 20 years later.

Also in 1976, the Conference secured an A.W. Mellon Foundation grant to fund a special workshop on the Appalachian Greenway concept, the pursuit of which was being transferred from the ATC to the revitalized Appalachian Highlands Association. Two months later, a new AHA board was elected, with Zoebelein as vice president, Murray as secretary, and former Vermont Governor Philip H. Hoff as chairman. However, before that board could meet again, Hoff resigned to direct the Coalition to Save New York City, AHA President F. Dun Gifford of Massachusetts left to head up Jimmy Carter's presidential campaign in New England, and active work on the proposal lapsed.

THE APPALACHIAN TRAIL BILL

About this time, the Trail's friends in Congress, alerted by reports from Conference members—especially such vocal advocates as recent thru-hiker Ed Garvey of the PATC and the ATC board—began to express concern over both the rapidly growing multiple threats to the footpath and the slow pace of governmental land acquisition to protect it. The federal agencies and Conference officials were called to testify at congressional oversight hearings on implementation of the 1968 National Trails System Act.

The Forest Service reported that it had added 117 miles of protected Trail within its boundaries. The National Park Service had made no significant progress, although an A.T. Project Office had been quickly formed in the North Atlantic regional office in Boston in March 1976, after the Trail community's discontent began to manifest itself at the Boone meeting. That office

OPPOSITE: Ed Garvey and Ray Gingrich, both Potomac Appalachian Trail Club members, hike in May 1967 in the southern mountains. ABOVE: The Trail through ferns above Sherman's Creek on East Mountain, Massachusetts.

worked on better relationships with Forest Service field-level officials. It continued to resist land purchases as the best approach to protecting the Trail, but the department did announce that it had set aside $1 million in emergency, 50 percent matching funds for one year to encourage states to buy some of the 374 miles of Trail on private land.

Paul Pritchard told the annual meeting of the Maine Appalachian Trail Club that the Trail was "facing a staggering increase in both hiker use and development pressure," wrote Bob Cummings, then a reporter for the *Portland Press Herald* and after retirement a leader in the club and the Maine A.T. Land Trust. Private lands "are being shifted from family farms to large corporations seeking housing subdivisions and commercial developments."

While several states had portions of the Trail protected within state lands prior to the statute, only Maryland, Massachusetts, New Jersey, Pennsylvania, and Virginia had noticeably responded to the federal statute's encouragement to lead the way on protection with protective statutes and / or acquisitions of their own. The political connections of officials in those and other states helped in other ways, both locally and nationally. Maine's Herb Hartman, for example, was determined to play a major role in protection in that state. And, in New York, Nash Castro—key to the development of the 1968 act—was more than halfway through a second career as executive director of the Palisades Interstate Parks Commission, basically the post Major William Welch held when the Trail project began, with important ties to the state leadership and influential philanthropists.

In early 1977, Executive Director Paul Pritchard was appointed assistant director of the Interior Department's Heritage Conservation and Recreation Service in the new Carter administration, and Henry W. Lautz was promoted to the top staff position. Later in that year, the Interior's passivity evaporated. At the member meeting at Shepherdstown, West Virginia, a dozen miles from the new ATC headquarters, keynoter Robert L. Herbst, recently appointed assistant secretary for fish, wildlife, and parks, in the strongest of terms promised renewed federal vigor in protecting the A.T. Back at his Washington office, David M. Sherman of that year's Georgia "Peanut Brigade"—later an ATC board member and briefly head of the NPS A.T. office—was doing the staff work to back that up, the beginning of a long career of enthusiastic, hard-charging dedication to securing the corridor forever.

The Park Service and ATC were soon at work drafting the amendments to the 1968 act they thought necessary to achieve permanent security for the resources. As those efforts went forward in Washington, the board members, as the federally designated coordinators of the A.T. in their states, were asked by the Park Service to choose a *preferred* route and corridor and to supply the names, addresses, and telephone numbers of the affected landowners, a task accomplished by volunteer teams on a crash basis.

In October 1977, the U.S. House of Representatives adopted amendments to the 1968 statute that came to be known as "the Appalachian Trail Bill." The Senate enlarged its scope the following February, the House accepted the changes, and President Jimmy Carter signed the legislation into law on March 21, 1978.

ABOVE: Annapolis Rock, just off the Trail in Maryland.

THE LAND-MANAGEMENT ERA BEGINS

At the time the amendments were enacted, slightly fewer than 1,250 miles of the Trail, or about 59 percent of the official route, were on public property: 775 miles protected by U.S. Forest Service acquisitions, 261.4 miles by states, and 213.5 miles by the National Park Service (primarily in the Great Smoky Mountains and Shenandoah national parks).

The central thrust of the amendments was an acceleration of the Interior Department's land-acquisition program to protect the A.T. Congress authorized $90 million for this purpose (with a portion to be actually appropriated each year) and extended the range of the program's eminent-domain authority to an *average* of 125 acres per mile, five times the maximum allowed by the original act. That $90 million is equal to more than $297 million today, less than the agencies have actually spent in acquiring more than 99 percent of the designated lands.

For corridor acquisition as a whole, the legislative history behind those amendments shows congressional intent that the width be expanded from roughly 200 feet to about 1,000 feet, a

---

"The Trail is a community of hikers enjoying the beauties of nature, and sharing concerns, blisters, adventures, sore toes, sprained knees, and the wonders of a wild country. It's two 20-year-olds jogging to catch Solo Sal, a 62-year-old retired school teacher who had left her tent poles behind. It's an 80-year-old retired grocer in North Carolina offering a hiker from Maine 'a ride to the top of the hill.' Some hike alone, others with friends, lovers, relatives—or strangers met a few moments or a few days earlier on the Trail. All share a common experience, a common adventure. All join in each other's successes and tribulations, share meals when supplies run low, and lament the mishaps and illnesses. Trail registers are filled with words of encouragement for those left behind. Like the hay mowers on Robert Frost's New England hill farms, the people who hike the trail, hike together, 'whether together or apart.'"

—BOB CUMMINGS, retired newspaper reporter, thru-hiker, in a 2009 post on Trailplace.com

---

yardstick developed a few years earlier as a result of a University of Pennsylvania landscape-architecture study of the Trail. Moreover, the legislative history explicitly recognized the active role of ATC volunteers and instructed the agencies to maintain their close working partnerships with volunteer-based organizations involved with the Trail. The amendments also reinforced the statutory standing of the Appalachian National Scenic Trail Advisory Council (ANSTAC), a body with federal, state, and ATC representatives to provide guidance to the secretary of the interior.

The National Park Service moved its new A.T. Project Office to Harpers Ferry in the fall of 1978. David A. Richie, the deputy regional director in Boston who had staffed it there, was named manager. A former Navy pilot and former Marine captain with a law degree, Richie had a long and varied Park Service career behind him. Until he acquired government-leased space three blocks away and began to build a small staff, he worked at the ATC's office alongside David N. Startzell, the nonprofit's number-two staff member, a planner a year out of graduate school who had arrived at the beginning of the year, as the amendments were being finalized in Congress. Over the next decade, the two would become a relatively quiet but persistent ATC–NPS tag team for the "corridor," perhaps not unlike the Avery–Ballard pairing for the "Trailway" of the 1930s–40s. The agency also established a land-acquisition headquarters 20 miles away in Martinsburg, West Virginia. Its national land-acquisition chief, Charles R. Rinaldi, took over as director of this effort, which became the most complicated one in the service's history.

Title-search work began on 1,750 privately owned tracts along the Trail. A flexible process was instituted to identify the best corridor locations in advance of purchase or easement negotiations. It used the cooperative management, or partnership, principles that were as old as the Trail itself, informally binding public officials, ATC, and club volunteers and the neighboring landowners in common cause.

The goal was, and is, to have the Trail off roads and in as natural a setting as possible, preferably at the height of land. The width of the corridor or buffer zone would vary, but, outside the boundaries of the six national parks and eight national forests with Trail mileage, it averages about 1,000 feet in most states—depending on the particular topography, vegetation, boundaries of developed property, and the availability of alternative, undeveloped lands.

Most of the land was acquired by outright fee-simple purchase. Where an owner wished to continue farming, grazing livestock, or producing timber in ways compatible with the Trail concept, the whole range of available tools—from easements to lease-backs to reserved interests— was used to try to meet the multiple interests involved.

Sometimes, the federal agencies could not acquire a parcel (or move quickly enough), but a significant natural, scenic, historical, or cultural resource needed to be protected in a hurry. Facing a western-oriented bias against public landownership on the part of the new Ronald Reagan administration's political appointees as well, the ATC in 1982 created a new program, the Trust for Appalachian Trail Lands, maintained wholly with private contributions, to acquire such property for the corridor or facilitate other forms of protection. (In 1999, the program's name was changed to the ATC Land Trust, and after 2005 it became part of the conservation department.) That administration's interior secretary, James Watt—reviled by most outdoors organizations— still conferred the department's highest award for conservation service on Ruth Blackburn, the ATC's chair from 1980 to 1983 and a tireless worker before and after in researching land titles and contacting landowners in northern Virginia and Maryland.

The 1979–80 acceleration in land acquisition after a decade's delay prompted considerable discussion within the project leadership about the future role of volunteers vis-à-vis the government agencies. It had begun stirring in 1968, with the shift away from an all-volunteer administration for the Conference as some of the realities of the initial legislation became apparent. Now, with teeth (and money) in the statute, the ATC had to face this third era, although it would be five more

years before the answer started—and *only* started—to become more clear: What exactly should the Conference, and the volunteers at its center, be doing if the federal and state governments now had the primary responsibility for locating and protecting the Trailway/corridor?

CHANGES IN LEADERSHIP

As added conduits for information and opinions among the Conference, the agencies, and the clubs, the ATC in 1978 and early 1979 established regional field offices in New England, Pennsylvania, and Tennessee. (In the 1980s, the southern region was split into two areas: one for central and southwest Virginia and a second for North Carolina, Tennessee, and Georgia.) The Conference also began publication of *The Register*, a special volunteer-edited newsletter for volunteer maintainers.

Chairman George Zoebelein stepped down in August 1979 after a four-year tenure, and Charles L. Pugh of Richmond, Virginia, was elected to succeed him at the members' meeting in Carrabassett, Maine. Pugh resigned slightly more than a year later, between meetings, citing internal board disagreements, particularly over finances and staffing, as well as the competing demands of work and family.

Ruth Blackburn, of Bethesda, Maryland, who had been involved with the Trail and the Conference since the 1930s and was mid-Atlantic vice chairman at the time, and Jim Botts of Lenoir City, Tennessee, the southern vice chairman (who had taken Startzell on his first volunteer work trip when he was a graduate student at the University of Tennessee), became acting cochairmen. Blackburn was elected in November 1980 to lead the Conference for the rest of Pugh's term.

Also at that November 1980 meeting, Laurence R. Van Meter of Vermont, a former executive director of the Green Mountain Club, resigned his board seat to accept his colleagues' offer to become the new executive director, effective February 1, 1981, succeeding Henry Lautz, who had resigned in May. Startzell, who would become associate director under Van Meter, was acting executive director for that transitional period.

In the early 1980s, the Conference concentrated on increasing its membership, developing with the NPS the legally required comprehensive and land plans for management of the Trail and Trailway, conducting its own internal long-range planning, and maintaining both the appropriations for Trail-corridor acquisitions and the working partnership with the federal agencies entrusted with the privately developed Trail as a public resource under the act.

Those efforts—the entire process of redefining the roles of the partners, with the ATC at the hub of the wheel—culminated not only in a stronger internal organization and blueprint for the future but also in an agreement unique in the annals of American public-land management. It paralleled the unique nature of the land-acquisition program for the Trail.

That three-page agreement, to which a longer, detailed memorandum was attached, immediately became known as the delegation agreement, although officially known as Amendment No. 8, National Park Service Cooperative Agreement No. 0631-81-01. It reaffirmed for all parties the

OPPOSITE: Virgin's bower, a showy clematis native to the southern mountains, graces Max Patch, a landmark maintained "bald" just inside North Carolina from Tennessee in the Pisgah National Forest—a major acquisition for the Trail after years of persistent efforts by the Carolina Mountain Club's Arch Nichols.

leadership role of the *private* volunteer in the stewardship of the Trail, even though it had become a *public* resource under the 1968 act.

This third ATC era—the land-management era—would be overlaid on the tasks of Trail work established in the first stage of the project and Trailway-protection efforts established by the second.

The Typical A.T. Hiker

Capturing Sasquatch would be easier than describing the typical Appalachian Trail hiker. As imagined and constructed, the Trail is used most often by people out for a short summer's walk, an afternoon of bird-watching, a stroll on a crisp fall day with the sound of crunching leaves as the only distraction, a commute to work through a wildlife refuge or historical park the Trail bisects, or an hour or so sitting on a rock looking out across a valley and inward as far as one can go. The Appalachian Trail has no entrance exam or demographic qualifiers, although "dreamers" is the label used most often, when one can get away with labeling.

Some have hiked the whole Trail in less than 60 days, one as quickly as 46. Some have taken as long as 46 years. Most simply go when they can and want. A few merely see a sign while driving across

the mountains, jump out of the car, walk 10 yards, and then gleefully blog about being "just once" on this legendary strip of rocks, roots, dirt, and winding staircases to views beyond imagination.

Even the one in 1,000 in any given recent year, the aspiring thru-hiker who gets all the attention, cannot be pegged, although some generalizations are fair and white men still dominate. (That's changing, too, though.) The ages have ranged from eight to 84 or more; the conditioning, from hypertoned to doughboy; the backpacking experience, from none to 10,000 miles. Most hikers are "in transition": just out of school, just retired (especially from the military), in between jobs or marriages. Every dot on the political, occupational, and income spectrum is covered someplace along the footpath—and is mostly irrelevant.

In one of the larger shelters, you might be sleeping with a retired admiral, a Cherokee chief, a Tidewater town policeman on his vacation, a Chapel Hill publisher, a perpetual Trail maintainer so far out of the mainstream he doesn't even have a Social Security card, a suburban woman waiting to hear back about her bar exam, a friar, and a Pennsylvania mechanic taking a few days off work. In a tent nearby, there might be a soldier or Marine who spent all his downtime in Afghanistan reading A.T. books he ordered online from the ATC.

Most of these long-distance hikers go on to something else. Some have gone on to found such companies as PC Connections or return to work as the CEO of Whole Foods. Some just keep hiking—literally, by turning around and going the other direction, or heading home to short-term jobs to collect enough money to return to the Trail next year. ATC records—and they are known to be incomplete—show that two dozen people have hiked the Trail more than five times, a few more than 10. More than 200 have hiked it three times.

These long-distance hikers are the most studied (yes, more than a few theses and dissertations are on the shelves), because they can be found and tend to be the ones writing the books, getting in the newspapers and magazines, and chatting online. The late Dr. O. W. Lacey, a psychologist at a Pennsylvania university who finished the Trail in 1980 after a decade of section-hiking, collected Myers-Briggs questionnaires from more than 800 hikers and found that introverts were twice as common among long-distance hikers as within the general population, even as Trail use grew and the culture became "more social."

Flipping through 90 years of photographs of hikers and maintainers on the Trail (or what became the Trail), the parade of clothing, gear, and hairstyles is as predictable as it is entertaining. Flipping through more than 60 years of written memoirs—ranging from short to very, very long—leads to a remarkably different observation. For all the ways in which the insular Trail and its world has changed, for all the changes in the escaped world apart from it, when these writers do allow a little sentiment to slip in between all the advice and daily logs of food and landmarks and mileages, the feelings they express today echo all the way back to those first short walks in the woods past a metal diamond or a white blaze.

Backpacking gear has slimmed way down from the mid-twentieth century (opposite). A recent hiker climbs a stile over a fence (right). One man, Bob Barker, thru-hiked the Trail with crutches (below left). All finishing northbounders celebrate atop Katahdin's Baxter Peak (below middle), and daytime breaks have been staples forever: witness these 1927 hikers on the Long Trail/Appalachian Trail in Vermont (below right).

Flora

The rich diversity of plant life on the eastern
mountains not only provides visual treats for
the hiker but also puts the Appalachian Trail
in the top 10 for natural resources among the
more than 380 units of the national park system.
Hundreds of rare, threatened, and endangered
species are seldom seen except by experts.

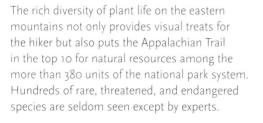

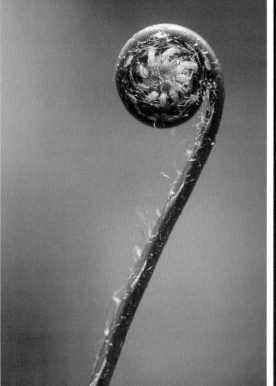

CHAPTER 6

Redefining the Mission, Reshaping the Trail

On January 26, 1984, with Secretary of the Interior William P. Clark looking on, National Park Service Director Russell E. Dickenson signed over to the Conference the responsibility for managing in the public interest the lands acquired by the agency for the corridor, as well as for maintaining the footpath itself. "Our signatures on this agreement evidence faith on the part of government and private partners alike that extensive public lands can safely be entrusted to a private organization," said Dickenson.

The document was signed on the mezzanine of the American Institute of Architects headquarters two blocks from the White House, as a tribute to the teamwork of Benton MacKaye, *AIA Journal* editor Clarence Stein, and Charles Whitaker in developing and promoting the original A.T. concept more than 62 years earlier.

Secretary Clark commented: "Without its great volunteer tradition, there would be no Appalachian Trail nor would there be such widespread support for its preservation as a part of our national heritage. The Appalachian Trail Conference and its committed volunteers have earned the trust of the American people."

Volunteer management of the Trailway, from boundary gates or signs to preservation of cultural and other resources within it, "will be a sizeable task,

the magnitude of which may not yet be apparent, and will require a higher degree of responsiveness than many clubs may be used to. We welcome the challenge," said Don Derr, then president of the New York–New Jersey Trail Conference. The dimensions of this *official* stewardship responsibility would not be fully perceived for years, but the main thrusts were clear.

Corridor management not only embraces disseminating information and devising ways to ensure access to the Trail for all types of users, it also means verifying boundary lines in the field and meeting such threats to the resources as logging, dumping, and all-terrain vehicles. It has also come to mean taking inventories not only of bridges and other facilities to be maintained, but also rare, threatened, and endangered species (and invasive species encroaching on the lands) and historic and other cultural resources within the Trail's lands.

And, while law-enforcement and fire-control authorities could not be delegated by the park service or the states, an obligation to establish and oversee procedures for bringing the authorities to the trouble spot could be and was. The arrangement also meant the ATC's adhering now to the same rules and procedures a regular national-park staff would have to follow in all aspects of its work. For example, before removing some incompatible structure on a piece of land acquired for the corridor, it had to expensively test for and remove asbestos rather than, say, giving the local fire department a training spot and a pack of matches.

Under the pact, the ATC guarantees to the National Park Service that the Trail and Trailway are being well cared for. To fulfill its obligation at the immediate level of the resource itself, the ATC redelegates to the clubs with Trail-maintaining assignments the additional responsibility of corridor management. But, in doing so, in consultation with all parties, it develops and publicizes standards, as well as policies, for Trail and Trailway design, protection, maintenance, and use. The clubs develop local management plans intended to spell out how those standards will be applied in their particular areas and how disagreements will be resolved (generally through regional committees, but occasionally at the board level).

Putting together the foundations of this new era for the A.T. and the Conference—developing local plans, assessing corridor resources, refining procedures, and broadening the base of governmental partners—became the focus of the organization's work, even as the land-acquisition programs and all other aspects of the project continued.

STEADY HIKING RATES AND A NEW DIRECTOR

Despite a few dips during the gasoline-shortage years, Trail use for long-distance hikes was steadily climbing. The number of completed hikes in a year never fell below 100 after 1978. By the end of 1986, the registry held 1,404 hikes. It had crossed the 1,000 mark in 1981, the same year multiple thru-hiker and teacher Warren Doyle—no less gregarious than Ed Garvey but much more the rebel—formed the Appalachian Long Distance Hikers Association with a few dozen of his fellows. It remains the only established "users' group" for the Appalachian Trail.

PREVIOUS SPREAD: Katahdin rises as a monolith out of the Maine woods above Daicey Pond.
ABOVE: Charlie's Bunion, an outcropping in North Carolina left after a fire and storm, named by Horace Kephart.
OPPOSITE: Looking out from Dragons Tooth in central Virginia, south of Catawba.

Midway through 1986, Van Meter resigned to return to school en route to a new career in educational administration. On November 8, the board selected Dave Startzell as the next executive director. Chuck Rinaldi, the land-acquisition chief, reflected recently that Startzell's appointment "was a classic example of the right person for the right position at the right time. Prior to the appointment of Dave as director, ATC had undergone two directors in fairly short succession. There was considerable sentiment for the appointment of a director who would bring stability to this leadership position. When Dave was appointed, there was considerable 'water fountain' talk as to whether this was the right selection. It took only a very short amount of time for the 'water fountain' talk to turn very positive."

Startzell, for his part, was focused on what he was best known for: securing federal appropriations to acquire the remaining lands and joining with Dave Richie and Chuck Rinaldi and their Forest Service counterparts to negotiate the tougher purchases and design a "win-win" route across them.

The remaining challenges of the land-acquisition program were considerable as Startzell assumed the directorship. Could he sustain his record of securing between $8 million and $11 million a year in Land and Water Conservation Fund appropriations for the park- and forest-service A.T. lands programs? More attention couldn't hurt, but it, too, had to be managed.

A cover-blurbed article in *National Geographic* magazine in February 1987 kicked off the 50th-anniversary year for the Trail itself; its readership, in the millions, generated well more than 10,000 requests for information. Widely publicized celebrations of the anniversary were principally organized by a thru-hiker from Conyers, Georgia—Dan "Wingfoot" Bruce—including the inaugural Trail Days in tiny Damascus, Virginia, which now draws upwards of 20,000 participants each May. All that led to a two-year, 25 percent surge in membership and uncountable new hikers out on the Trail, testing a decade's worth of "hardening" and special footpath designs intended to stand up to the inevitable next wave of hiking and backpacking enthusiasts. That 2,000-Miler registry—the gauge of Trail use, tiny sample that it is—more than doubled in size, from 1,700 reported hikes by 1986 to 3,687 by the end of 1995.

Securing appropriations the agencies would spend as fast as they made their way to their offices proved not enough to clear the hurdles left in the acquisition program. In Vermont, for example, even intervention by U.S. senators and state officials and full-throttle direct-mail and media efforts by both sides did not move the question forward of a permanent route for the Trail between (or within) the Killington and Pico ski lands. The ATC had to sue its primary partner, the National Park Service, for negotiating a closed-door deal with the owners of the Killington resort. The ATC then arranged for congressional intervention and hearings. That led to extended mediation sessions, announced agreements, failures to close, and more talks—but, finally, success and an end to the controversy in December 1997.

"The A.T. reminds us of our simple past as a country and of our basic simplicity as a people."

—DAN "WINGFOOT" BRUCE, 1987, *The New York Times*

In the Cumberland Valley of Pennsylvania south of Harrisburg, use of eminent domain became necessary in a few cases, as it did in less than five percent of the total parcels involved in the complicated project. Eventually, the route—public meetings about and arguments over which had consumed the 1980s—was put in place: off the roads and onto farm fields and ridges. Then, the Trail community had to set about rebuilding relations with the communities and bringing the farmers back to work the land, all to maintain the rural landscape amid rapidly developing interstate sprawl. As they did in parts of Virginia, hikers would have to include in their repertoire climbing stiles over barbed wire, strolling along rows of corn, and keeping cows (and bulls) at a safe distance.

OPPOSITE: Early trail workers working their way across a stile built to get hikers across fences without the risk of freeing livestock.

Not too far to the north, where the Trail passes from New Jersey into New York, was the 20,000-acre Sterling Forest, the European owners of which filed plans for intensive development right on top of the Trail corridor. An energetic coalition of the New York–New Jersey Trail Conference, ATC, AMC, and other groups in the metropolitan area began to move. It took most of the decade, but, in the end, the governors of both states went to their legislatures in the name of their watersheds, the Trail community went to Congress, and Sterling Forest is now a state-managed public park.

Those were "the big ones," the preparation for the last and perhaps toughest one: securing a satisfactory permanent route across Saddleback Mountain in western Maine against the opposition of the absentee owner of that ski area, who was backed by property-rights activists from the West and the Maine congressional delegation.

The ATC's land-trust program, which had facilitated the saving of the Trailside namesake lake of Boiling Springs, Pennsylvania, went on to previously unthinkable projects: preservation of an 18th-century farmstead abutting the Trail corridor in southwestern Massachusetts; protection of a 1,600-acre property tying the Trail corridor to the Shenandoah River in northern Virginia; and expansion from a staff of one into a corps of 14 contract coordinators on the lookout for land and experiences to preserve. At the turn of the century would come its most ambitious project: preserving the 4,000-acre Mount Abraham and associated properties to the east of the contentious Saddleback section in Maine, a nearly two-million-dollar effort.

DAVE STARTZELL'S START AS DIRECTOR

The Conference went into the 1990s with a membership of nearly 24,000 individuals or families, total assets of $2.58 million—a gain of 150 percent in just three years—and a "net worth" of more than $2 million: a position of strength, it thought, for tackling the costly, demanding, and still not fully defined challenges of its responsibilities under the 1984 agreement.

Dave Startzell began with 18 employees, two-thirds in Harpers Ferry and the rest scattered among the four regional offices. He knew that was not enough, but also wanted any growth in staffing to track with development of the right infrastructure throughout the public-private partnership and better emotional bonds among those partners. In his first speech as director to the membership, at its biennial meeting in Lynchburg, Virginia, he put forth what he saw as the challenges:

> In 1937, our members and leaders hardly took notice of the fact that we had just achieved what many believed to be the impossible—clearing and marking the world's longest continuous footpath. Instead, they were busily crafting a new vision—the concept of an Appalachian "Trailway"—a protective corridor of publicly owned land extending the length of the Trail, to provide a permanent right-of-way and to preserve the extraordinary range of natural and cultural resources along the Trail's route.

OPPOSITE: Children's Lake, the centerpiece of Boiling Springs, Pennsylvania, and a stop on the antebellum Underground Railroad, was acquired along with its shoreline for the Trail in the 1980s through a joint effort of the ATC land trust, the National Park Service, and a local philanthropist.

Today, that great vision is very close to being a reality. In the next three or four years, an Appalachian "Trailway" will exist from Maine to Georgia.

But, where do we go from here?

I believe we must view the Trail as a "backbone" for a much broader "conservation zone." Hopefully, we can serve as a catalyst for sensitive land use and recognition of significant resources well beyond the narrow confines of the Trail corridor . . . .

We are just beginning to realize the complexities of land management. It is an awesome task. And yet, I believe we can establish a very high standard of care, for the Trail and for Trail lands, based almost entirely on volunteer stewardship.

It is both a challenge and, in a sense, an obligation. We have an opportunity to demonstrate that there are few limits to what can be achieved by a dedicated and well-organized network of volunteers . . . .

The Trail should become, first and foremost, a "classroom" for learning about our environment and our unusual approach to resource management. Our "students" should include all of our visitors—both those who make a journey of five million footsteps and those who can experience only a fleeting glimpse from a single overlook or a few moments of solitude in the forest . . . .

Startzell, who came to the project in his late 20s, shared with the pioneers that enduring allegiance to the idea of contributing something "distinct . . . to the American recreational system," an answer he gave in some variation every time someone asked why he did what he did for the last 34 years. It was as constant as the appearance in his speeches—to the membership and countless others elsewhere—of the words "obligation," "responsibility," and "opportunity."

He came to the project as a volunteer—in the spring of 1974 as a graduate student in planning at the University of Tennessee, heading into the woods above the Nantahala River at Wesser, North Carolina, with Jim Botts and Arch Nichols. After Nichols died in 1989, Startzell wrote, "I began to realize [that day] that people like Arch Nichols represented a very special breed . . . . It was, for me, a dawning of appreciation for both the 'body' and the 'soul' of the Appalachian Trail project. And, I wonder to this day how many other people Arch infected with his love of the outdoors." It was something they brought equally to bear on their Trail work.

Before his selection as director, Startzell took on an array of projects. They ranged from creating a 10-foot-long relief map of the Trail that remains the signature item in the thrice-renovated headquarters visitors center (duly noted by Bill Bryson in *A Walk in the Woods* and sought out by many tourists because of that) to serving as hands-on "general contractor" for rehabilitation of the Bears Den hostel property the ATC acquired above the Shenandoah River in Virginia in the 1980s.

The Dave Startzell–Dave Richie tag team lasted less than a year into his directorship, but Chuck Rinaldi stepped seamlessly into that role for two years after Richie retired in the summer of 1987. Donald King succeeded Rinaldi at the lands office. By 1995, the project office had been renamed the A.T. Park Office, and Pamela Underhill, daughter of one of the Bureau of Outdoor

Recreation officials who drafted the reports that led to the 1968 statue, was named park manager after 15 years working there. Throughout the next 16 years, Startzell constantly said they were "joined at the hip."

Startzell testified every spring before a House appropriations subcommittee, almost always with a volunteer from the board sitting next to him. Later joined by conservation-staff members and as part of a coalition of Washington-based groups seeking Land and Water Conservation Fund monies, he led a squad of volunteers on congressional office visits, armed with briefing packets that detailed both landmarks acquired and land sought in each state.

National Park Service wariness was no longer a problem, and the Forest Service was just as willing as it had been, although not always able. The greater urgencies came from the general economy. From the late 1980s to the late 1990s, the NPS alone protected more than 500 miles of the Trail, but land prices overall had more than doubled—in some states, much more—and more than 100 miles were still vulnerable.

Yet, that overarching land-acquisition goal from the organization's earliest years still had to contend for attention and energy with direct threats each year, also driven from the general economy—highway projects, powerline and other utility right-of-way crossings or parallel visual intrusions, military overflights and artillery exercises, and telecommunications towers sprouting like spring weeds. The latter required a two-year, ATC-led effort to raise the consciousness of that industry to its impacts on an older American recreational experience.

BELOW: Hiker wandering in the primeval-feeling woods of Maine.

THE POWER OF VOLUNTEERS

The ATC expanded volunteer crew programs in all regions to help clubs meet the challenges of moving the footpath onto the permanent locations the acquisition program secured and of adjusting overnight-shelter supplies to the new demand. While some locations necessitated numerous public hearings to gain local landowner satisfaction, others spawned resistance from hikers. But the law says "scenic trail" for a reason, and that means going to the ridgetops. Almost every decision now involved federal lands or federal money, so reams of environmental-impact and regulatory-compliance reviews became parts of ATC and club life. Yet, room remained for the spectacular: Trail bridges across the broad James River in Virginia and deceptively sleepy Pochuck Creek and its broad swamp in New Jersey were both multimillion-dollar projects with many private, state, and federal partners that were actually executed far beyond the original dreams.

The ATC even, in a manner of speaking, geared up to meet the challenges of nature. The enormous mid-Atlantic damage of back-to-back hurricanes and winter or spring floods in the late 1980s and 1990s was repaired, and the Trail reopened, in a matter of weeks each time. Fittingly, the secretary of the interior in 1996 *started* a publicity walk across the Potomac River from the Harpers Ferry ATC headquarters to gain congressional support for rebuilding funds for the Chesapeake and Ohio Canal towpath after hurricane flooding destroyed many sections. Somewhat awkwardly, he had to walk past ATC volunteers who were *wrapping up* their repairs of the A.T. section, a cooperative effort of the Conference, the local club, and two other units of the national park system, underwritten by a corporate member.

Those recoveries were among the more dramatic testimonies to the fact that the Trail project is no longer a matter of fewer than 200 high-energy volunteers but instead a product of the work of 6,000 volunteers giving more than 200,000 hours a year just in on-the-Trail work—hand in hand with federal and state workers in nearly every endeavor except basic maintenance. To maintain the resources to support and train these volunteers, Startzell created in 1990 a stewardship endowment with a $100,000 challenge grant from a small family foundation. Although tapped heavily in 2005 for reorganizations and infrastructure investments, by 2012 it had net assets of slightly more than $2 million, less than what Startzell intended "to get us away from living hand to mouth," but still double the whole ATC operating budget at the time he took over.

The Stewardship Fund grew to $2.5 million in its first decade, coming in 2000 to represent a third of the organization's $7.5 million or more in total assets. Membership had risen, too, after sitting on a plateau for most of the 1990s, to top 30,000 by the ATC's 75th anniversary in 2000. The staff had grown as well, to nearly 50 year-round employees, backed by a dozen seasonal workers during the spring, summer, and fall.

The acquisition side of the Trail project meant not just securing funds. It meant redesigning and reconstructing much of the official 1971 route and corridor, which had to be amended from time to time, not only in location but also in the amounts of bordering land that would be needed to ensure, for example, a view that seemed to define the statute's values. Taking that official route

OPPOSITE: The only U.S. chief executive to visit (much less work on) the Appalachian National Scenic Trail, President Bill Clinton helps Vice President Al Gore place a capstone in April 1998 on a trailside wall next to Jefferson Rock in Harpers Ferry, West Virginia.

down to the level of individual parcels (nearly 3,000 in all) meant sometimes-rowdy local public hearings for Startzell, his NPS management partner, and the NPS land-acquisition chief. A quarter century or more later, some of the communities that initially opposed a "government takeover" of a strip of land were among the first to seek the ATC's help in economic development or other political efforts and to seek the cachet of designation as an A.T. Community™, a program the organization initiated in 2009.

Sometimes the rowdiness was not so public. Within the Manhattan commuting area, for example, those mountain tracts were choice properties for celebrities, which drove up the prices. Some, such as singer James Taylor, readily agreed to a riverside scenic easement in New England. A broadcast psychologist in New York, on the other hand, took her complaints directly to the NPS director; that one took a while to resolve without lawsuits.

The addition of the Trail to the national park system also meant an official comprehensive management plan in 1981 that begat more plans for all partners and a land-protection plan, all of which Startzell had a hand in crafting. As the route would change in small degrees constantly, not only more paperwork was required, but also a decision-making process that required "optimal location reviews," an on-the-ground process developed by the Forest Service, ATC, and local clubs to choose the best spots, given both the Trail's values and local realities. Every time a forest or

park had to redraw its own management plan or go through the environmental-review process for a particular action, more often than not it was Startzell going through those reams of paper to ferret out the potential effects on the Trail. Then, he would draft official comments supporting or opposing the plans.

In 1998, President Bill Clinton, fresh from an hour of Earth Day Trail work with Vice President Al Gore, publicly threw his voice behind the land-acquisition effort in remarks from The Point—a ledge in Harpers Ferry above the confluence of the Potomac and Shenandoah rivers— and the end of this era really did seem near. A few weeks later, Representative Ralph Regula of Ohio, chairman of the appropriations subcommittee, called Startzell from the House cloakroom to report proudly that all the remaining federal funds requested to complete protection of the corridor were approved and the bill was on its way to President Clinton.

Alas, the end of the acquisition was not quite the case. Some major projects in New England were added to the desired NPS inventory. Forest Service funds kept getting taken for forest-fire suppression, and its lands staff kept being whittled down. In several cases, by the time it could begin negotiations on a major tract, prices had soared yet again in the years of the housing bubble that burst in 2007. Startzell stopped asking for a general Appalachian Trail line item from the Land and Water Conservation Fund appropriations, themselves being chopped year after year, but he did go back with his crew each year to try to fund a handful of projects at a time.

Today, fewer than six miles of Trail remain "unprotected," much of that in one central Virginia section above the New River that has been in negotiation for years. The rest are mostly sections crossing municipally owned watersheds, which cannot be purchased but where conservation easements can permanently protect the Trail's values as well as the city's.

The most satisfying of the acquisitions? Shortly before he retired in early 2012 at age 62, Startzell said it was the corridor for the Trail across Saddleback Mountain in Maine, after two decades of bitter battles with the owner of the ski resort there. Those battles were carried out at local hearings, within the Maine congressional delegation, inside the NPS environmental-impact proceedings, and in the news media (and the ATC's fund-raising letters). Just as the offensive easement that precipitated the lawsuit over the Killington route in 1989 was signed on the last day of the Reagan administration, the Saddleback issue was headed for decision in the last weeks of the Clinton administration in 2001.

The Maine interests behind the Boston-based owner of the ski resort brought in former Senator George J. Mitchell Jr.—an occasional diplomatic troubleshooter for Clinton—and the Startzell–Underhill tag team was left waiting at home as the decision arena moved up the ranks of the Interior Department. Even though it was an "imposed settlement" that overruled the long-developed NPS / ATC position, "we ended up with a pretty decent corridor . . . at a truly magnificent spot I had walked many times," Startzell said.

Perhaps it is fitting that land acquisition never truly, completely ends, just as trailblazing has never truly, completely ended since it began in 1922. Certainly it was typical that the organization and its major partners already had their hands in yet another mission for the project.

OPPOSITE: Sign atop Maine's Saddleback Mountain, which, with its panoramic views and alpine meadows, was the last major jewel in the $200 million A.T. acquisition program shepherded by Dave Startzell. He termed it the most satisfying after a two-decade battle that went all the way up to the Cabinet level.

ABOVE: Former ATC Executive Director David Startzell (right) with ATC Chair J. Robert Almand (left) after 2010 congressional briefings.

Protecting the Trail

In January 1979, the National Park Service bought an 11-acre parcel on the east side of Hosner Mountain Road in Dutchess County, New York, for the Appalachian Trail—the first drop in an acquisition storm that followed Congress's 1978 mandate to get moving to protect the rest of the Trail.

A decade later, half the Trail states together had purchased land to protect more than 114 miles, and the U.S. Forest Service had added more than 440 tracts totaling more than 46,000 acres surrounding 843 miles within national-forest boundaries. The Chuck Rinaldi–led NPS team had made up for lost time: 1,776 parcels secured 522.6 miles of the Trail with 79,624 acres of buffer in 11 states. Under Donald King in the 21st century, it secured almost all the remaining 100 miles. But it is the landmarks brought into the Trailway, not numbers, that tell the acquisition story:

MAINE

- Portions of the Barren–Chairback range, more than 31 miles across White Cap and Moxie Bald mountains and the summits of North and South Crocker, as well as Crocker Cirque
- The shorelines of three Great Ponds and undeveloped Nahmakanta Lake, as well as more than three miles along Pierce Pond Stream
- The entry to spectacularly rugged Gulf Hagas
- A two-and-a-half-mile corridor across the panoramic summits of Saddleback Mountain, one of the state's most valued alpine zones

NEW HAMPSHIRE

- A 13-mile stretch through the super-rugged Mahoosuc Range, outside the reach of state and White Mountain National Forest lands that protected about two-thirds of the Trail
- A new route between Smarts Mountain and Mount Cube
- Mount Cube and Mount Hayes, the bookends of the White Mountains
- The dramatic overlook of Holts Ledge, which allowed successful reintroduction of peregrine falcon nests in 1988

VERMONT

- To protect the half of the A.T. not within the Green Mountain National Forest, NPS bought more than 5,200 acres to eliminate roadwalks near towns, protect wooded settings, and secure the nearly roadside Thundering Brook Falls
- The Forest Service went after 36,000 acres on Glastenbury and Stratton mountains, the former to become a designated wilderness
- A wooded route between the newly merged Killington and Pico Peak ski resorts, the highest A.T. points in the state

MASSACHUSETTS

- Jug End Mountain, literally overlooking the southwest corner of the state
- The surprisingly remote Upper Goose Pond and the upper reaches of Connecticut-bordering Sages Ravine
- The 400-foot-high Cobbles rising above the valley near Cheshire

CONNECTICUT

- A corridor along virtually the entire western shore of the Housatonic River
- The summits of Lions Head and Bear Mountain
- The confluence of Housatonic and Ten Mile rivers along the New York border, leaving for a two-decade court battle a three-parcel stretch above it on Schagticoke Mountain

NEW YORK

- Half the Trail in Dutchess Country and a third in Putnam moved off roads and into woodlands along lakes and across small summits
- What began as securing a narrow passage around Little Dam Lake led to protection of the entire 20,000-acre Sterling Forest

NEW JERSEY

- Additions to the state corridor to allow space for shelters and to protect significant wetland and agricultural environments
- Pochuck Mountain and Pochuck Creek, the latter to later be crossed by an engineering marvel

ABOVE LEFT: McAfee Knob on Catawba Mountain, Virginia; ABOVE RIGHT: Steps up Max Patch in Pisgah National Forest, North Carolina.

PENNSYLVANIA

- A 16-mile greenbelt across the A.T.'s longest—and most development-threatened—valley crossing, including Children's Lake in Boiling Springs, the headwaters of Yellow Breeches Creek
- The approaches to the Susquehanna River near Harrisburg and the Delaware River at the New Jersey line

MARYLAND

- Filling in the gaps of a continuous state park across the ridge of South Mountain between fast-growing Frederick and Hagerstown

VIRGINIA

- More than 30 miles of roadwalks eliminated even as a ragged path of plots had to be woven through a congested I-81 interchange
- Such outcroppings as McAfee Knob, protected as a small part of a difficult acquisition of several thousand acres centered on Catawba Mountain and Tinker Ridge
- A 2,800-acre buffer between the Blue Ridge Parkway and the growing Wintergreen Resort, and, in time, a new ascent to Peters Mountain from the New River at Pearisburg
- Chestnut Ridge, with its sweeping view of Burke's Garden below, and a ribbon throughout Sinking Creek Valley, a major eastern watershed divide

WEST VIRGINIA

- In addition to about two miles wholly within the state, about 23 miles straddling the boundaries with Virginia in two spots

NORTH CAROLINA AND TENNESSEE

- Several thousand acres on the Roan Highlands, Hump Mountain, and many nearby balds, plus Grassy Ridge
- Laurel Fork Gorge and the lower end of the Nantahala River Gorge
- Eight miles above Hot Springs, North Carolina
- A 400-acre section centered on open 4,629-foot Max Patch

GEORGIA

- A broader corridor in spots where second-home developments were springing up along the footpath in gaps

Footbridges and Towers

Some observation towers remain along the Trail from the days before airplanes became better at spotting fires. Some state highway departments erect bridges across busy highways, while volunteers in clubs—sometimes with federal or state agency help—provide the way across steep ravines and broader rivers. Then, the occasional monument comes into view.

CHAPTER 7

New Challenges, a New Trailway

At the end of 2000, then-First Lady Hillary Rodham Clinton named the Appalachian Trail one of 16 national millennium trails, recognizing its place in American cultural and recreational history. The Trail itself seemed flooded with people that year—partly the result of "world-coming-to-an-end" fever and partly the cumulative effect of Bill Bryson's *A Walk in the Woods*, which is what hikers are still talking about as their inspiration to try walking the Trail's whole length.

The book was published in hardcover in 1998 (first in Great Britain, then in the United States) and in paperback in 1999, with the audiotape quickly following. Completed end-to-end hikes of the Trail had already jumped from the 200s per year in the early 1990s to more than 400 per year from 1996 to 1998, and that total went up to 557 in 1999. In 2000, the ATC estimated an unprecedented, 45 percent surge from 1999 in the number of people starting out on thru-hikes.

The 638 reports for that year were not exceeded until 2011—not because the number of those attempting has grown, but because those attempting are generally more successful. The rule of thumb before 1990 was that one in 10 would make it all the way to Katahdin or Springer Mountain; today, it is better than one in four, as the amount of hiking advice available has exploded.

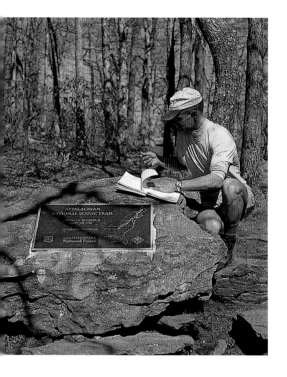

With the growth of the Internet, especially chat rooms and other interactive sites, the ATC is no longer the only source of Trail information as sought by the insatiable, long-distance dreamers, although it remains the source of official information, guidebooks, and maps. Where only a handful of how-to books and hiker memoirs were on the shelves in 1990, 200 or more are available now. Every major outdoor retailer chain in the East sponsors a series of thru-hiking workshops or clinics, as do several smaller shops and a few enterprising former thru-hikers. The number of 2,000-Miler reports passed the 8,000 mark in 2004 and the 12,000 mark seven years later.

Plus, the footpath itself continued to slowly grow as the ever more "final" relocations prompted by the land-acquisition program were opened. That 1937 Trail of an estimated 2,049 miles, which slipped to 2,000 miles by 1951 with the major Virginia shift away from the lower Blue Ridge Parkway, was measured in 2000 at 2,167.1 miles with almost no complaints about Trail conditions coming in to the central offices of the project.

The Trail was in place, stable, and well used. What had been called the Trailway since the late 1930s and was now termed either the corridor or the management zone, depending on the lead agency, was essentially in place. But, there was still "an elephant in the room" that went beyond growing concerns from a frustrated Trail-management community—both volunteer and paid—that "we are constantly doing more with less" to meet National Park Service standards and ideas.

"If we ever forget that the Trail is our reason for being as an organization, we are in deep trouble," Chairman Raymond Hunt wrote in a year-end message to ATC members in 1987. "That is a simple statement, but one that is vital to [our] success—past and future." It was fondly cited forever after as "Ray's Rule" whenever an initiative was thought to stray into broader, if politically popular terrain. But, it was found not to be sufficient in defining either the desired Trail experience or the ATC's core responsibility in the 21st century.

REPAIRING THE RELATIONSHIP BETWEEN THE ATC AND TRAIL CLUBS

Slightly more than two months after Dave Startzell started as education director at the ATC, President Jimmy Carter signed into law amendments to the 10-year-old National Trails System Act, the statute that brought the footpath into the national park system as a national scenic trail and authorized acquisition of lands to protect it. Those ATC-sought amendments added teeth to the original authorization and approved a wider land buffer. They also authorized more money and reestablished the volunteer-based ATC's role in its care. Within its legislative history—and a number of documents and compacts to follow—was a clear deal with Congress: the ATC would manage to the highest standards the land Congress agreed to protect with taxpayers' dollars.

But securing the funds—including some from private sources funneled through the small land trust the ATC established in 1982 when all public-lands projects were threatened—was but

PREVIOUS SPREAD: View from Mount Eisenhower, White Mountain National Forest, New Hampshire. ABOVE: Prospective thru-hiker signs the register that goes inside the boulder atop Springer Mountain, the southern terminus of the A.T. OPPOSITE: More than 2,000 miles away, a hiker crosses the rooftop of Maine.

one piece of one prong of a two-pronged challenge posed by the 1978 amendments and accepted by the ATC. That double challenge with its many pieces, and how Startzell responded, would come to define the ATC's work and nature today.

Once the amendments were law, then-Chairman George Zoebelein called the only "special meeting" of the board on record, in the spring of 1978, to start planning "what it's going to take" to meet that obligation . . . as if everyone knew then exactly what the obligation meant in day-to-day terms.

"There were some disconnects . . . . Relations weren't great at that time" with the clubs, which were brought under that obligation by the ATC, Startzell said. Other than a mostly social meeting every few years, club and ATC contact was minimal, and some club leaders admitted that they sought a seat on the board just to find out what it was that the ATC did. A certain commonality of purpose had to be restored with clubs and agency offices outside Washington, D.C. The ATC needed to become relevant again as a real force for the Trail as a whole—not as a meeting planner, but as the essential hub of an ever-more-elaborate wheel in motion.

Regional offices were created to provide a presence "in the field," along with *The Register*, a volunteer-edited newsletter for maintainers. Trail crews, volunteer-training programs, and a grants-to-clubs program were instituted, and a biennial club-presidents meeting was held from the mid-1980s into the 1990s. Other outreach followed, including detailed management-planning guides, mile-by-mile Trail assessments, and resource inventories to generate five-year work plans.

The latter would eventually feed an NPS planning process that led to new funding, largely gathered and distributed by Pam Underhill after she became manager of the A.T. Park Office, although relatively smaller amounts had begun with the signing of the 1984 agreement. The funding, under contracts, became considerable—about $1.5 million a year now from different parts of the NPS budget—but, even today, it covers only a third of the direct Trail-related work of the ATC, although it represents 25 to 30 percent of the annual budget for the nonprofit.

APPALACHIAN NATIONAL SCENIC TRAIL ADVISORY COUNCIL

Somewhat behind the scenes in the 1970s, the now-little-remembered Appalachian National Scenic Trail Advisory Council (ANSTAC)—a creature of the 1968 National Trails System Act meant to guide the secretary of the interior in policymaking—was working as something of a shadow ATC governor. A central body with all states, the major agencies, the ATC, and a selection of clubs represented, it worked on those "What is it going to take?" and "What do we do now?" questions.

ANSTAC deliberations largely framed the contents of what is officially known as Amendment No. 8, "the delegation agreement" under which the ATC assumed responsibility for the care of all A.T. lands acquired by the NPS, now more than 100,000 acres of the roughly 275,000 for the whole corridor. At the time, the ramifications of its provisions were less than fully understood.

ABOVE: Sages Ravine forms the state line for the Trail between Connecticut and Massachusetts just east of the New York line.

Startzell helped support ANSTAC's work for the last half of its 20-year existence. One of its chairmen, Charles H. W. Foster—a former president of The Nature Conservancy and Yale University forestry-school dean—described Startzell as "planner, amateur ornithologist, and, reputedly, the most consummate technician on the staff."

It was a good disguise for a chief executive who later tried to hire good people, expected them to do their jobs, and let them, while he went about his mostly external-relations projects—stepping in only if something vital stalled. Not that Startzell ever stopped being a copious note-taker; writer of detailed, analytical, suggestive memos; craftsman of on-the-mark budgets; or believer that the "e" in "e-mail" stands for "exhaustive."

"To experience the A.T. is to get to know the soul of America and what we value deeply, to experience the places we have chosen to permanently protect and preserve. Americans have a longing for wildness and a nostalgia for the landscape of our fathers, where the mountains were forested, farms dotted the valleys, and signs of modern technology and all the stress that comes along with the fast-paced life it engenders is absent. Anyone who can walk can hike the Appalachian Trail. You needn't be an athlete to hike the Appalachian Trail, and you don't need technical gear or advanced orienteering skills. There is nowhere else on Earth I know of where an ordinary person can spend six months immersed in nature, long enough that it can become a life-altering experience. One learns how few material goods one needs to survive and be happy and yet how much we humans are social creatures bound to each other."

—LAURIE H. POTTEIGER, a 1987 thru-hiker, in a 2011 magazine article

---

Early on in the process of building up the volunteer-based ATC management force, a top NPS park superintendent who also had been part of the ANSTAC planning, in his keynote at the first club-presidents meeting in 1985, said, in effect, "You will fail. You have no idea what it takes to run a park" as envisioned by the delegation agreement. As superintendent, he was responsible for slightly fewer than 200,000 acres with a staff of 136—seven-and-a-half times that of the ATC at the time—and a base budget of $13.5 million—13 times the ATC's.

Challenge accepted. The resources and skills of the entire ATC network needed to be raised to that level. The corps of skilled, mostly highly educated volunteers needed to be trained to the new expectations. More employees needed to be brought in to facilitate that and, in part, to buffer volunteers from federal requirements. That role was and is shared by the initially one-person NPS office (ATPO). Today, the ATPO has about a dozen employees.

Annual revenue has increased at more than three times the rate of inflation, and income flows from more than a dozen sources now instead of three. The ATC has been debt-free for more than 16 years, and net assets have increased at more than five times the rate of inflation. The total of $10.4 million in net assets includes 40 tracts of lands (two with significant historic structures) and 60 easements that the ATC staff has to maintain and monitor.

Startzell would take credit individually for hardly any of that; it was *always* "we," usually referring to a volunteer leader or agency counterpart or a manager on the staff. As he told members at his last ATC meeting, in July 2011 at Emory & Henry College in southwest Virginia, "The reality is that none of the achievements of the past 30-plus years can be fairly attributed to me or to any one individual. ATC is a big, far-flung, and sometimes-unruly extended family, but it is only through our collective action that we have been able to achieve so much. I simply had the good fortune to join the staff of ATC at a critical juncture in the evolution of the organization and the Trail project."

THE APPALACHIAN TRAIL CONSERVANCY

Nonetheless, greater dependency on federal funds was not all good—it made it harder to secure private funds, and their continuance is always in some doubt. The ATC's leadership also felt the work was unfocused and the organization's identity was clouded as well. Successive chairs after Raymond Hunt—Margaret Drummond from Georgia, a volunteer since the 1970s, and David B. Field from Maine, a volunteer since the 1950s, who both came on the board about the time Startzell came on the staff—had initiated "strategic planning" efforts that in time bogged down in paper and charts. In late 2002, Chair Brian T. Fitzgerald pushed the process into action.

A "summit meeting" of all management interests in the Trail, public and private, was convened for three days in May 2003 to try to narrow to a handful the priorities of the project. By that fall, consultants and the ATC–ATPO leadership successfully proposed a reorganization of the staff with sets of specific goals for each program area. They also floated the idea of a change in name to better capture the land-management focus rather than leave the focus on umbrella guidance and the biennial meetings they thought "conference" implied. A year later, the leadership successfully proposed that, in July 2005, the Appalachian Trail Conference become the Appalachian Trail Conservancy.

Just as "Trail" shifted to "Trailway" in the 1930s, the shift from Conference to Conservancy signified that the health of the lands through which the footpath meanders had to be the primary concern of the organization if it hoped to preserve forever the experience many millions had already drawn from walking through its nooks, for whatever amount of time, for eight decades. As a matter of fact but not general recognition, the footpath and shelter sites together comprise *only one-quarter of one percent* of the lands in the ATC's care.

Volunteer-based Trail maintenance—keeping the footpath open and safe, with shelters and bridges to meet the needs of users—continue to be met by the able 31 independent local clubs, some of which also picked up tasks associated with monitoring a corridor with more than 4,000 miles of boundary. The ATC continues to support those volunteers with tools, training, and ever-more-modern means of communicating with each other.

OPPOSITE LEFT: A pupil whose teacher is a part of the ATC's new Trail to Every Classroom program enjoys the Trail. OPPOSITE RIGHT: ATC staff members install major rock steps down to Jefferson Rock in Harpers Ferry, West Virginia, one hot August morning.

Key to both prongs for the long term would be recruiting a new generation of volunteers from a younger generation of hikers and neighbors, both on rural lands and within the more than 100 towns within five miles of the Trail. Within five years, several efforts in that direction were launched, with two moving quickly to the forefront through the 14 states: Trail to Every Classroom, a joint ATC/NPS effort to train up to 50 teachers a year in ways to incorporate the Trail into their curricula (and entice children onto the Trail with the hope they would grow into volunteers, too); and the Appalachian Trail Community program, which designates towns and counties along the Trail as such, helping them with economic development efforts, tapping new sources of volunteers to help with "their backyard," and setting the framework for friendly local land-use policies. (In Pennsylvania, landmark legislation late in the first decade of this century required townships to adopt Trail-friendly policies—and provided some funds for the ATC to help draft them.)

The final pieces of the acquisition agenda would be relentlessly pursued—along with pieces just outside the corridor but within the "viewshed," as the opportunities and the funds arose. So, too, would the organization continue to be the source of official information and services to hikers outside the clutter of Internet-based sources.

Conceptually, the shift to trail conservancy was not such a grand leap. Accepting the delegation agreement had been interpreted for some time as "doing all the things a national-park staff would do" except law enforcement and regulatory decision-making. However, the magnitude

of the treasures—much less what it would take to care for them and enhance their situations, all the while enhancing the hiking experience—was of a far higher order than many had thought, even while they had made the case for acquisition of a meaningful corridor.

The United States has more than 370 "units" in its national park system. The longest and skinniest, the Appalachian Trail, had been identified as a "natural resource park"—and, when the initial surveys and studies came in, was found to probably harbor more rare, threatened, and endangered species than any other. Most of those species are plants—surveys of mammals and other animals are incomplete—and the Trail lands were found to support more than nine listed by the federal government as rare, threatened, or endangered and 360 listed by states. More than 80 of the species are globally rare; some are found only along the Trail. More than 2,050 populations of rare, threatened, or endangered plant species alone have been found in communities at 515 sites within the footpath's narrow buffer. Surveys of bird populations so far have been spotty, but the highest concerns have already been voiced about the fate of Bicknell's thrush in New England, with declining populations of certain woodpeckers, warblers, and flycatchers also noted.

Many see the Appalachian Trail corridor—the regenerating, ancient eastern forests that are among the most diverse of all in temperate zones—as a protected migratory path for many species. The correct habitat is the keystone for all species, and the corridor has no magic wall to guard against invasive species or other encroaching harm. Clean air—the kind you see free of smog and the kind you don't see free of ozone—is crucial to the life cycles within each habitat and the whole, which is home to more than 6,000 plant species, hundreds of birds, and more than 50 species each of amphibians, reptiles, and mammals, not to mention—on the right day in the right place—millions of insects.

Ice ages and glaciers left behind in the high-elevation southern Appalachians and the New Hampshire–Maine ranges cool-weather "island" environments that hikers and other observers have long said "should be in Canada." Certain habitats, such as montane spruce-fir forests, that are otherwise uncommon can be dominant for long stretches of the Appalachian Trail in the north and the south. The only alpine areas—with their rare vegetation—in the eastern part of the national park system are those within the Trail corridor in New Hampshire and Maine. The alpine plant community of the White Mountains' Presidential Range—one of the most-favored of all A.T. hiking experiences—is the largest and most diverse of the alpine areas in the Northeast, according to a summary of federal studies seeking to identify the most important environmental issues for the A.T.

More than 120 million people live and work downwind from the Trail. More importantly perhaps, nearly 1,800 streams, rivers, and lakes along the path naturally collect water and feed it into 64 major watersheds along the East Coast and Piedmont—the life force for people, agriculture, and fisheries. As it naturally collects water, it also collects airborne pollutants crossing the ridgecrests and dropping onto the footpath below.

That brief tally of the natural resources on Trail lands is only a start. As the remnant of the colonial frontier, the height of land, and the bisection of key trading routes, the lands also are home to the full or partial ruins of native American settlements, Revolutionary and Civil War skirmish

ABOVE AND OPPOSITE: Look down, look up in the Great Smoky Mountains National Park—clintonia and trillium on the forest floor to hardwoods reaching out of the mist.

and battle sites, Underground Railroad "stations," and early industry. That cultural inventory is yet to come, but already some officials are investigating whether the whole park belongs on the National Register of Historic Places.

What does that mean for the volunteer-centered caretakers? Soon after the change in name, an array of government agencies and academic interests saw the Trail corridor as a near-perfect early-warning laboratory for a range of environmental changes. The ATC and the Park Office coordinated the formation of a coalition of those scientific agencies and interests to receive and analyze the data for forwarding to policymakers at all levels.

In the end, the ATC would have to manage the impacts of those environmental changes and policy decisions as central to its charge to care for those lands. It would take on the tasks of recruiting "citizen scientists" to monitor the water and air and plant and animal species and send the data on—a wide-ranging environmental-monitoring effort known as the A.T. Megatransect, which brings together scores of governmental agencies and dozens of university and nonprofit

"On the Appalachian Trail, the traveler never knows what the next experience will be or where. It is the Unknown and the Unexpected that lures the hiker on."

—ELMER L. ONSTOTT, 1968

scientists. (Finding and yanking up exotic invasive species choking all the natives proved a great way to attract youngsters.) It also would seek new ways to educate the Trail's visitors to the impacts they had on those environments—and how they could help.

The magnitude of the new task seemed to far outweigh the magnitude of the organization's earlier (and continuing) tasks: putting a footpath of more than 2,000 miles on the ground, keeping it open and safe and beloved for everyone who seeks backcountry recreation on foot, and encasing it in a buffer of land owned by the American people. But people probably thought the same in the 1920s, the 1930s, the 1960s.

Before he retired, Dave Startzell had hopes that ATC membership would soon grow rapidly to the task, but acknowledged that organizational and footpath stability and the lack of threats to the Trail's continuity—which helped attract members from the 1960s through the rest of the last century—requires different lures. Today's threats are threats to the integrity of the land itself and its resources, "and most people find it hard to understand the needs and challenges of stewardship."

In January 2012, the board hired architect Mark J. Wenger—a volunteer active in two clubs, a 2,000-Miler, and longtime director of facilities at Colonial Williamsburg, where he worked for 32 years—to pursue those and other goals as the sixth executive director.

OPPOSITE: Elmer L. Onstott, shown here in Great Smoky Mountains National Park, was a prolific photographer of the Trail in the 1960s and went on to hike the entire length.

Impacts of Climate Change on the Appalachian Trail

Before we can discuss how climate change will affect the A.T., we need an estimate of how much climate will change. Climate scientists are reluctant to predict future climate, because such predictions depend on future carbon-dioxide (CO_2) emissions, which depend on the path of human development. How many people will there be? How wealthy will they be? How much energy will they use, and what will be the source of that energy?

Also, there are many climate models, and while they all agree that human activities will lead to a warmer climate, they disagree on how much warmer, particularly when looking at small areas of the world. Climate scientists refer to their calculations of potential future climate as "projections" to indicate that they are dependent on a specific set of assumptions and a specific climate model.

Because of the huge amount of computer capacity needed to run global climate models, even the best of these models average conditions over 100-kilometer square areas (about 4,000 square miles). This approach is satisfactory for flat areas, but not for mountainous areas, such as those traversed by the A.T., where microclimates change over short distances. To overcome this limitation, a technique called downscaling has been developed. Downscaling takes the output of a global climate model, then solves the model for a limited, smaller area. The Nature Conservancy, the University of Southern Mississippi, and the University of Washington have developed a downscaling tool called Climate Wizard (www.climatewizard.org) that presents historical average climate (1951–2006) and the results of climate-model projections for areas in the United States as small as a five-mile square (25 square miles). Each Climate Wizard projection of future climate includes annual and seasonal average changes in temperature and precipitation.

The Nature Conservancy provided the Appalachian Trail Conservancy with the information necessary to run Climate Wizard for a band five miles on either side of the A.T. As an example of results, Figure 1 shows historical average annual temperature over the A.T.

The ATC considered two climate-change projections:

- a moderate case that assumes the best estimate of the impacts of CO_2 emissions on climate and a midrange estimate of future CO_2 emissions; and
- a more extreme case that assumes that CO_2 emissions have a one-third higher impact on climate than the best estimate and 25 percent higher CO_2 emissions.

These two cases do not define the full range of climate-change projections. Both higher and lower estimates of climate change are available. Both cases project the same pattern of a warmer, drier A.T. in 2041–2060, with the more extreme case showing larger changes than the moderate case. The more extreme case projects 2041–2060 annual average temperatures over the entire A.T. that are 2.5 to 4 degrees Celsius (4.5 to 7.2 degrees Fahrenheit) higher than the 1951–2006 historical average. Summer and winter temperature projections are similar to the annual average projection. If this projection is correct, the summer temperatures along the whole A.T. would be warmer than the historical average at the southern end of the Trail.

The more extreme case also projects drier conditions over most of the A.T. and severely drier conditions over the southern end of the A.T. From the Smokies south, the more extreme case projects 200 millimeters (eight inches) less precipitation per year. The loss of precipitation is more severe in the summer, with the Trail as far north as Vermont receiving less rainfall.

Water availability, which is determined by the amount of precipitation that falls and the rate at which it either runs off or evaporates, could become a serious problem. Higher temperatures mean more evaporation. Without a significant increase in precipitation, they would lead to more frequent drought conditions over the A.T.

The habitats of plants and animals are determined by temperature and precipitation. Plants and animals can respond to warming temperatures by migrating northward or to higher elevations. Animal migration is obvious, since animals are mobile. Individual plants and trees cannot migrate, but the range over which they can propagate can change. For both plants and animals, the ability to migrate is limited by the availability of routes that are not blocked by human development or other impassable barriers and by suitable habitats. The A.T. may create a corridor for plant and animal migration, but not a guarantee that they will find suitable habitats.

Changes in climate extremes—monthly high or low temperature, drought, or severe storms—would significantly impact the A.T. These impacts include:

- Warmer winters, which would extend the hiking season. However, many plant pests are kept at low levels because they are killed off by cold winter temperatures. Warmer winters would mean that insects such as pine borers would be more likely to survive.
- Hotter summers, which would make hiking the A.T. a more physically demanding activity.
- Drought, which would dry up the water sources hikers depend on and make backpacking the A.T. more challenging. It would also weaken or kill trees. Trees weakened by drought are more susceptible to insect attack. Finally, drought can affect the Trail directly, by making its treadway more susceptible to erosion.
- Ice storms, which can cause millions of blowdowns, some of which would block the Trail. Warmer temperatures mean that the region susceptible to ice storms would move northward.
- More frequent hurricane-force winds, which currently are unusual along the A.T. Moreover, the Trail is susceptible to erosion from the heavy rains that accompany these storms. Hurricanes draw their energy from the warm water of the ocean surface, and there has long been concern that, as the oceans warm, hurricanes will become more common and/or more intense.

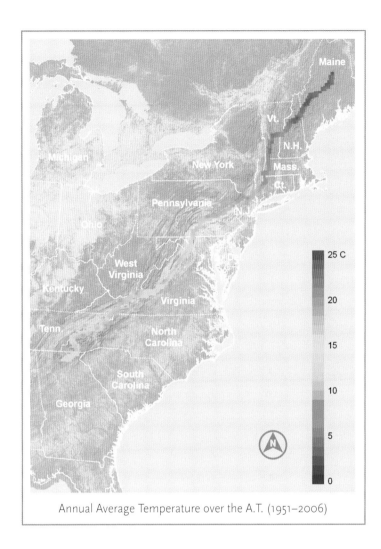

Annual Average Temperature over the A.T. (1951–2006)

- Warmer, drier conditions, which could increase the number of forest fires. Also of concern is the potential increase in fuel for these fires. The die-off of trees as a result of the change from boreal to northern hardwood forests, and increased blowdowns as a result of either ice storms or hurricane strength winds, could result in more intense, more destructive forest fires.

DR. LEONARD S. BERNSTEIN, a member of the Appalachian Trail Conservancy board of directors who has hiked the entire Trail, was a lead author of one of the chapters of the work of the United Nations Intergovernmental Panel on Climate Change that was awarded the 2007 Nobel Peace Prize.

Wildlife

Appalachian Trail lands are home to a wide array of birds, mammals, reptiles, amphibians, and insects—some endangered, most not, and (almost) all a delight to the visiting hiker.

Maine to Georgia

Maine

281.8 MILES

OPPOSITE: Katahdin, Baxter State Park
FOLLOWING SPREAD: The Tablelands
plateau atop Katahdin

ABOVE: Early-morning view of Katahdin; OPPOSITE: Daicey Pond, below Katahdin
FOLLOWING SPREAD: View of Katahdin from across the West Branch Penobscot River at Abol Bridge

PREVIOUS SPREAD: Above the Jaws, Gulf Hagas, just west of the A.T. (left); Katahdin (right)
ABOVE: East Carry Pond; OPPOSITE: Sandy Spring Pond with another view of Baxter Peak

PREVIOUS SPREAD: Saddleback Mountain near Rangeley (left); Screw Augur Falls in Grafton Notch State Park (right)
ABOVE AND OPPOSITE: Mahoosuc Notch, the hardest mile of the A.T.

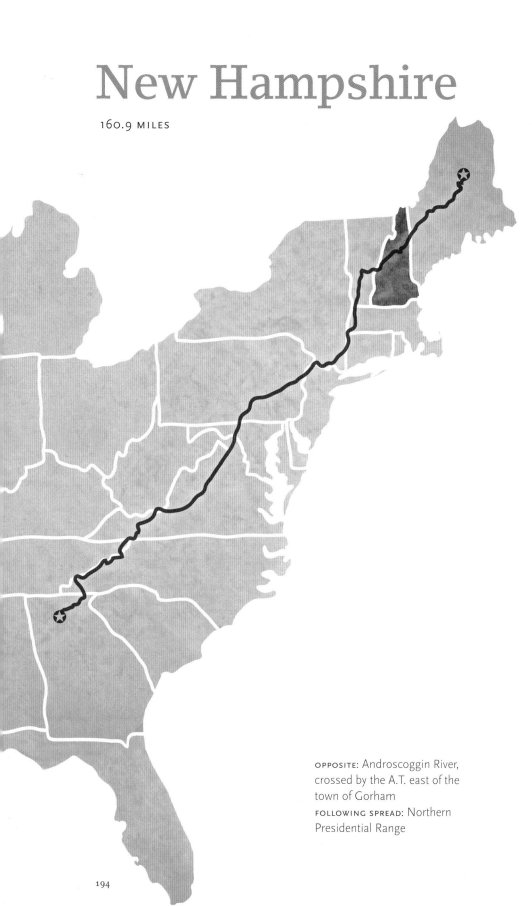

New Hampshire

160.9 MILES

OPPOSITE: Androscoggin River, crossed by the A.T. east of the town of Gorham

FOLLOWING SPREAD: Northern Presidential Range

ABOVE AND OPPOSITE: Approaching Mount Washington
FOLLOWING SPREAD: Mount Adams, reached by a side trail north of Mount
Washington (left); Mount Pierce/Clinton (right)

OPPOSITE: Webster Cliff Trail in the woods above the Saco River; ABOVE: Zealand Notch
FOLLOWING SPREAD: Little Haystack Mountain on Franconia Ridge (left); Mount Lafayette above Eagles Lake (top right); Lost Pond (bottom right)

OPPOSITE: Franconia Ridge above the Pemigewasset River; ABOVE: South Kinsman Mountain
FOLLOWING SPREAD: Brook through Franconia Notch State Park (left); Lonesome Lake (right)

ABOVE AND OPPOSITE: Mount Moosilauke

Vermont

149.8 MILES

OPPOSITE: Big Branch River near Danby
FOLLOWING SPREAD: Pine forest in Vermont
(left); Lye Brook Wilderness (right)

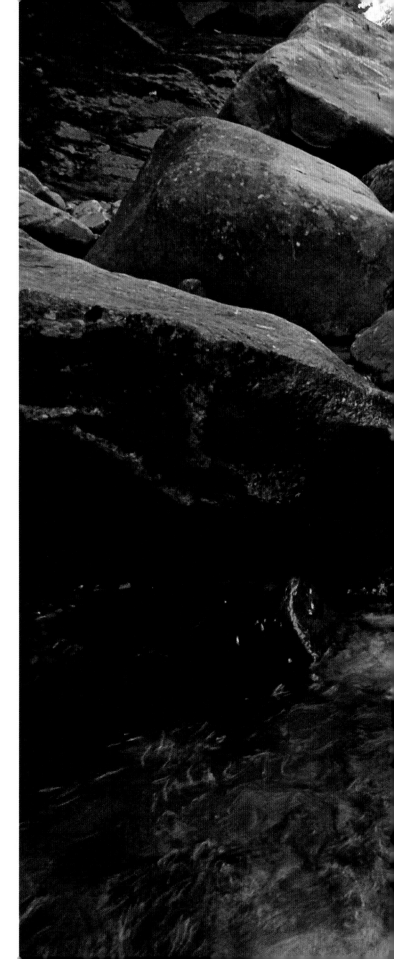

ABOVE: Stratton Mountain; OPPOSITE: Grout Pond, south of Stratton Mountain

Massachusetts

90.4 MILES

OPPOSITE: Upper Goose Pond
FOLLOWING SPREAD: Bear Rock Falls (left);
Sages Ravine (right)

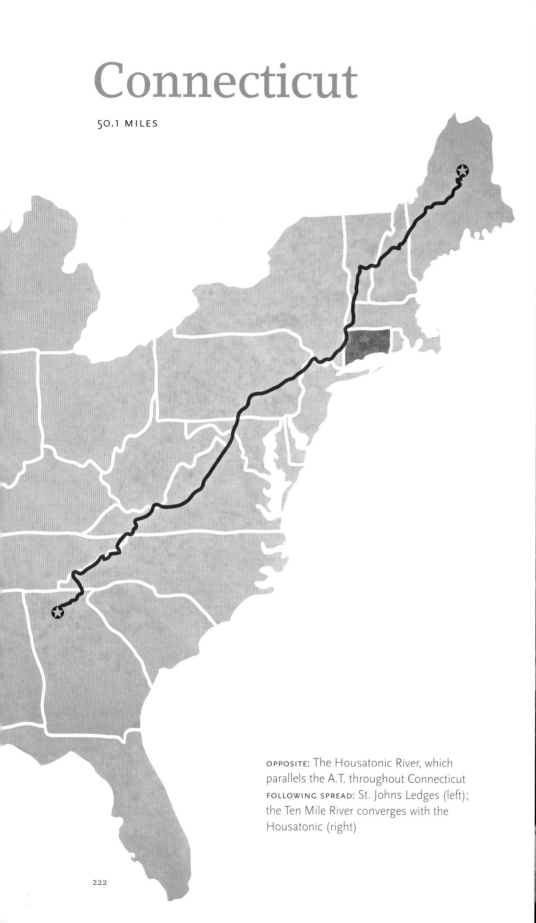

Connecticut

50.1 MILES

OPPOSITE: The Housatonic River, which parallels the A.T. throughout Connecticut FOLLOWING SPREAD: St. Johns Ledges (left); the Ten Mile River converges with the Housatonic (right)

New York

91.2 MILES

OPPOSITE: Bear Mountain Bridge over the Hudson River

OPPOSITE: Harriman State Park, near Island Pond west of the Hudson River

FOLLOWING SPREAD: Canopus Lake, Clarence Fahnestock State Park (left); Lemon Squeezer rock jumble (right)

229

New Jersey

72.2 MILES

OPPOSITE: A.T. in Stokes State Forest, above Lake Owassa
FOLLOWING SPREAD: A.T. in New Jersey runs through meadows (left) and relatively open forests (right)

OPPOSITE AND ABOVE: Sunfish Pond, Worthington State Forest

Pennsylvania

229.6 MILES

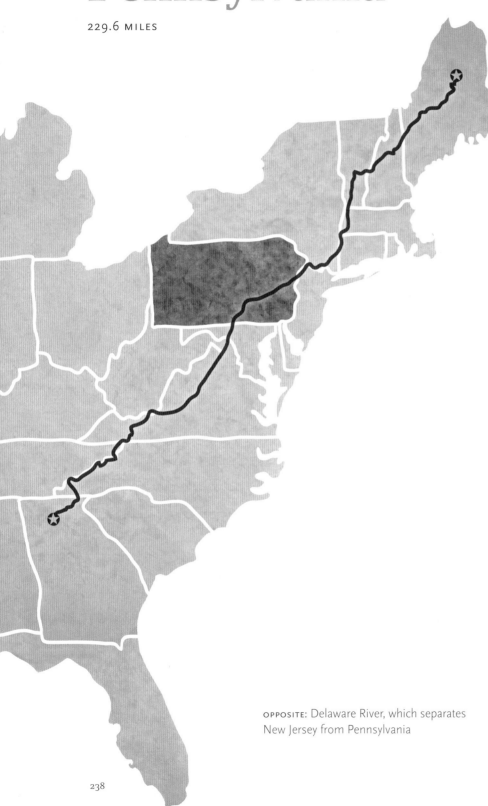

OPPOSITE: Delaware River, which separates
New Jersey from Pennsylvania

ABOVE: Bake Oven Knob north of Allentown; OPPOSITE: The Pinnacle
FOLLOWING SPREAD: View from The Pinnacle (left); Pulpit Rock (top right); Clarks Ferry Bridge across the Susquehanna River (bottom right)

ABOVE: View of the Susquehanna River from Hawk Rock on Cove Mountain; OPPOSITE: Hawk Mountain
FOLLOWING SPREAD: A.T. above Lehigh Gap (left); St. Anthony's Wilderness (right)

Maryland

40.9 MILES

OPPOSITE: Black Rock Cliffs
FOLLOWING SPREAD: Annapolis Rock

PREVIOUS SPREAD: Trail to first monument to President George Washington(left);
Washington Monument (right)
OPPOSITE: Potomac River and Weverton Cliffs; ABOVE: Potomac River near Harpers Ferry

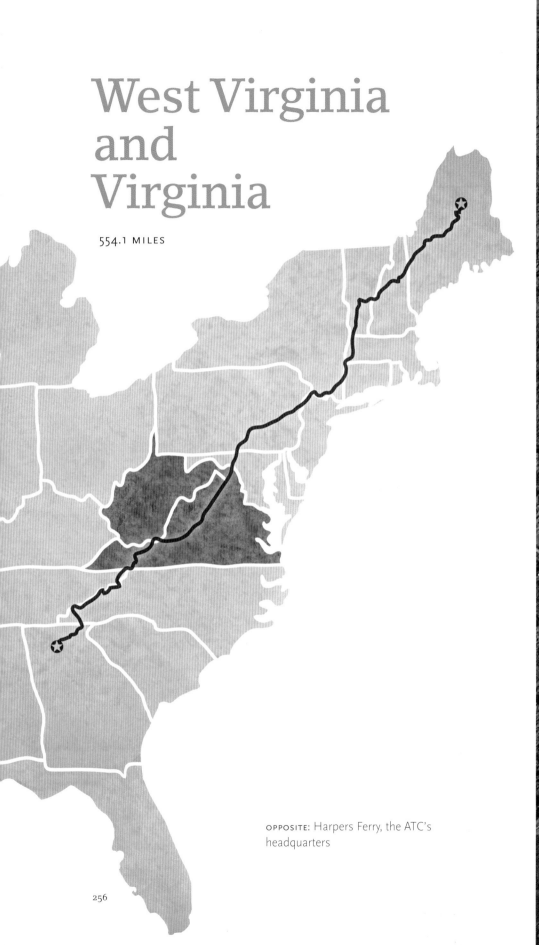

West Virginia and Virginia

554.1 MILES

OPPOSITE: Harpers Ferry, the ATC's headquarters

OPPOSITE AND ABOVE: Shenandoah National Park
FOLLOWING SPREAD: Shenandoah National Park

ABOVE AND OPPOSITE: Shenandoah National Park

OPPOSITE: Bearfence Mountain, Shenandoah National Park
ABOVE: Big Meadows, Shenandoah National Park
FOLLOWING SPREAD: Humpback Rocks above Blue Ridge Parkway

OPPOSITE: Reeds Gap; ABOVE: Overlook on The Priest; FOLLOWING SPREAD: James River Valley, Virginia

PREVIOUS SPREAD: Thunder Ridge
Overlook (left); The Guillotine (right)
OPPOSITE: McAfee Knob

PREVIOUS SPREAD: Dragons Tooth (left); beech forest south of Mount Rogers (right)
OPPOSITE: Elk Garden, south of Mount Rogers; ABOVE: The Scales, a former livestock holding and weighing corral

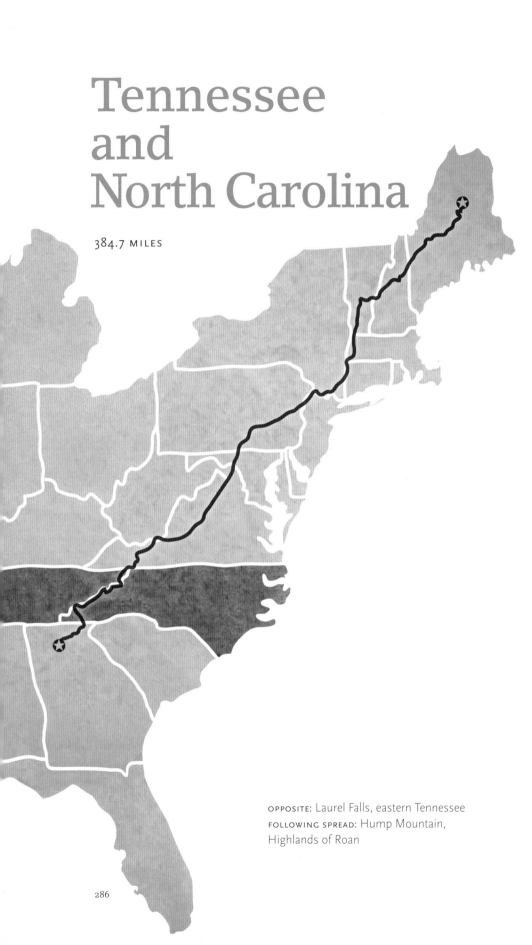

Tennessee and North Carolina

384.7 MILES

OPPOSITE: Laurel Falls, eastern Tennessee
FOLLOWING SPREAD: Hump Mountain, Highlands of Roan

OPPOSITE: Roan Highlands: ABOVE: Roan High Knob; FOLLOWING SPREAD: Jane Bald

PREVIOUS SPREAD: Grassy Ridge
ABOVE AND OPPOSITE: Above the Nolichucky River, eastern Tennessee

296

PREVIOUS SPREAD: Big Bald (left); Curley Maple Gap (top right); Street Gap (bottom right)
OPPOSITE: Big Butt; ABOVE: Camp Creek Bald

PREVIOUS SPREAD: Tanyard Gap (left); Mill Ridge (right)
ABOVE: A.T. along French Broad River; OPPOSITE: View of French Broad River from Lovers Leap Rock

PREVIOUS SPREAD: French Broad River (left); Bluff Mountain (right)
OPPOSITE AND ABOVE: Max Patch

OPPOSITE: South of Cosby Knob
FOLLOWING SPREAD: Eagle Rocks (left);
side trail to Mount Cammerer (right)

311

OPPOSITE: Footpath around
Charlie's Bunion
FOLLOWING SPREAD: A.T. through
the Smokies (left); Clingmans
Dome, Great Smoky Mountains
National Park (right)

PREVIOUS SPREAD: Fontana Lake
LEFT: Stecoah Gap, Nantahala National Forest
FOLLOWING SPREAD: Wayah Bald (left);
Albert Mountain (right)

Georgia

78.5 MILES

OPPOSITE: Springer Mountain

APPALACHIAN TRAIL APPROACH

SPRINGER MTN., GA. 8.5 MILES

MT. KATAHDIN, MAINE 2,108.5 MILES

PREVIOUS SPREAD: Springer Mountain; ABOVE: Approach trail to Springer Mountain, Amicalola Falls State Park; OPPOSITE: Amicalola Falls

Epilogue

BENTON MACKAYE GOT HIS "FOOTPATH OF THE WILDERNESS," ALTHOUGH LITTLE OF THIS backcountry is true wilderness and it would be difficult to argue that his would-be "Barbarian utopia" either repelled the metropolis or generated the waves of social betterment he envisioned as a result.

Myron Avery got his defined footpath on the ground and marked from his beloved Katahdin south to Georgia, although today hardly any of those miles he walked and wheeled—other than on Katahdin's approach—remain part of the Appalachian Trail, this very slim thread across the East's oldest mountaintops and valleys. Without suggesting he would ever be a satisfied man, it is not too hard to think he would be pleased that he and his anonymous volunteers and those who followed had, indeed, created "a distinct contribution to the American recreational system."

The leaders who followed—arm in arm with their tag-team partners of the National Park Service, U.S. Forest Service, and certain states in the shadows—protected the greenway and the path within and developed a corps of volunteer stewards unrivaled in the care of American public lands.

"The Appalachian Trail—the brainchild of a teen-ager, the product of generations of cooperation, one of our most precious national gems, the longest natural thoroughfare in the world, passing through four of seven forested habitats on North America, a haven for rare plants and animals," noted President Bill Clinton in an Earth Day address to Trail volunteers in 1998. "Thanks to many of you here today, the Appalachian Trail surely has surpassed even Benton MacKaye's wildest dreams."

Four generations of hikers have been able to retreat, if not escape, to the people's path, through a place the people protected for the future. One could argue that the Appalachian Trail project has come full circle. An unsigned, onion-skin document in the ATC archives—Clarence Stein is a likely author—dates from some time between 1921 and 1925. It states:

> The purpose of the Appalachian Trail is to stimulate what Chauncey Hamlin refers to as an "outdoor culture." This means the study of nature. And, it means the study of man. It means the study of man's place in nature. We have the physical features of the Earth, their geologic causes, and their economic consequences. We have the cultural features of the Earth, their historic causes, and their sociological consequences. We would plan for consequences through an understanding of causes.
>
> We would plan specially for America. And, we would seek her spirit through direct contact, not through printer's ink. The outdoor culture is a contact culture. It seeks first-hand access to the forces, natural and human, which underlie our country; it places no reliance on a prating journalism. The Appalachian highland (which is within reach of half the nation's population) forms a background, still unspoiled, of American tradition. Its crestline marks a natural backbone for an American outdoor culture.

OPPOSITE: Tar Jacket Ridge, Virginia

At the same time, ironically perhaps, preserving the people's path means that, after nine decades, the depressions and recessions and wars and political oscillations that could be barely acknowledged and then brushed aside—as a different world from the dream-catching Appalachian Trail project—must now be let in. The health of the Trail lands that is now the top—but not only—priority of the project is contingent on environmental forces in that other world. Economic and political responses could well determine what the Appalachian Trail becomes in its second 75 years.

In *this* century, protecting the Appalachian Trail experience requires more than buying a cocoon of land. Protection today means more holistic monitoring of *everything* going on in those woods and everything having an impact. We need to know more about the causes of changes to wildlife habitat and air and water quality to properly protect the resources behind that hiking experience, and those changes could be far-reaching. An army of volunteers is growing to help the Appalachian Trail Conservancy gain that knowledge and make wiser decisions from it. What is at stake is the *only* element of the people's path—sorry, Benton—that is honestly primeval: the magic of the eastern mountains.

Appalachian Trail Maintaining Clubs

MAINE APPALACHIAN TRAIL CLUB
P.O. Box 283
Augusta, ME 04332-0283
www.matc.org
The Augusta-based Maine Appalachian Trail Club maintains 267.2 miles of the A.T. from Katahdin in Baxter State Park to Grafton Notch at Maine 26.

APPALACHIAN MOUNTAIN CLUB
5 Joy Street
Boston, MA 02108
(617) 523-0636
www.outdoors.org
Founded in 1876, the Appalachian Mountain Club is America's oldest nonprofit conservation and recreation organization. It promotes the protection, enjoyment, and wise use of the mountains, rivers, and trails of the Appalachian region. The club's operations based at Pinkham Notch, New Hampshire, maintain the A.T. for 60 miles from Grafton Notch at Maine 26 to the side trail to Madison Spring Hut in the White Mountain National Forest and a second 60 miles from Edmands Col below Mount Washington to Kinsman Notch at New Hampshire 112.

RANDOLPH MOUNTAIN CLUB
P.O. Box 279
Gorham, NH 03581
www.randolphmountainclub.org
The Randolph Mountain Club's mission is to promote enjoyment of the Randolph, New Hampshire, area through hiking, trail development, upkeep of camps and shelters, and sharing the collective knowledge of its members. It maintains 2.2 miles of the A.T. from the side trail to Madison Spring Hut to Edmands Col below Mount Washington in the White Mountain National Forest.

DARTMOUTH OUTING CLUB
Dartmouth College
113 Robinson Hall
Hanover, NH 03755
(603) 646-2429
thedoc@dartmouth.edu
www.dartmouth.edu/~doc/
The Dartmouth Outing Club (DOC) is the oldest and largest collegiate outing club in the country. DOC maintains 53.3 miles of the A.T. from Kinsman Notch at New Hampshire 112 to the Connecticut River at Hanover, New Hampshire, the boundary with Vermont.

GREEN MOUNTAIN CLUB
4711 Waterbury-Stowe Rd
Waterbury Center, VT 05677
(802) 244-7037
gmc@greenmountainclub.org
www.greenmountainclub.org
Founded in 1910, the Green Mountain Club (GMC) maintains 149.8 miles of the A.T. from the Connecticut River on the New Hampshire border to the Massachusetts border near North Adams. The Trail coincides with the Long Trail for 105 miles through southern Vermont.

AMC–BERKSHIRE CHAPTER
at@amcberkshire.org
www.amcberkshire.org
The Berkshire Chapter of the Appalachian Mountain Club has more than 3,400 members throughout western Massachusetts. The chapter's A.T. Management Committee is responsible for maintaining and managing the 89.7 miles of the A.T. between Sages Ravine near the Connecticut line and the Vermont border outside North Adams.

AMC–CONNECTICUT CHAPTER
chair@ct-amc.org
The AMC–Connecticut Chapter Trails Committee maintains 52.3 miles of the A.T. through the Nutmeg State.

NEW YORK–NEW JERSEY TRAIL CONFERENCE
156 Ramapo Valley Rd
Mahwah, NJ 07430-1199
(201) 512-9348
www.nynjtc.org
Since 1920, the New York–New Jersey Trail Conference has worked with parks to create, protect, and promote a network of more than 1,700 miles of public trails in the New York–New Jersey metropolitan region. It maintains almost 162 miles of the A.T. from the Connecticut line near Kent to the Pennsylvania border on the Delaware River.

WILMINGTON TRAIL CLUB
P.O. Box 526
Hockessin, DE 19707-0526
wtcmembership@yahoo.com
The Wilmington Trail Club, based in Delaware, maintains 7.2 miles of the A.T. from the Delaware River at the New Jersey / Pennsylvania border to Fox Gap at Pennsylvania 191.

BATONA HIKING CLUB
www.batonahikingclub.org
The Batona (BAck TO NAture) Hiking Club of Philadelphia maintains 8.6 miles from Fox Gap at Pennsylvania 191 to Wind Gap at Pennsylvania 33.

AMC–DELAWARE VALLEY CHAPTER
dvchair@amcdv.org
www.amcdv.org
The Delaware Valley Chapter of the Appalachian Mountain Club offers day hiking, backpacking, canoeing, kayaking, bicycling, cross-country skiing, snowshoeing, winter mountaineering, trail maintenance, conservation cleanups, educational workshops, meetings, and programs throughout the year. It maintains 15.4 miles of the A.T. from Wind Gap at Pennsylvania 33 to Little Gap near Danielsville.

PHILADELPHIA TRAIL CLUB
m.zanger.tripod.com
Started in 1931 and based in the Delaware Valley of southeastern Pennsylvania, the Philadelphia Trail Club maintains 10.3 miles of the A.T. from Little Gap near Danielsville to Lehigh Furnace Gap near Ashfield.

BLUE MOUNTAIN EAGLE CLIMBING CLUB
P.O. Box 14982
Reading, PA 19612
info@bmecc.org
www.bmecc.org
The Reading-based Blue Mountain Eagle Climbing Club maintains 65.5 miles of the A.T. in two pieces, from Lehigh Furnace Gap to Bake Oven Knob and from Tri-County Corner to Rausch Gap Shelter, south of the northernmost crossing of I-81 and south of Pennsylvania 443.

ALLENTOWN HIKING CLUB
P.O. Box 1542
Allentown, PA 18105-1542
president@allentownhikingclub.org
The Allentown club maintains 10.7 miles of the Trail from Bake Oven Knob to Tri-County Corner.

SUSQUEHANNA APPALACHIAN TRAIL CLUB
P.O. Box 61001
Harrisburg, PA 17106-1001
www.satc-hike.org
The Susquehanna Appalachian Trail Club maintains 20.8 miles of the A.T. from Rausch Gap Shelter west of Pennsylvania 443 to Pennsylvania 225 northwest of Harrisburg.

YORK HIKING CLUB

president@yorkhikingclub.com
www.yorkhikingclub.com
The York Hiking Club has one or two activities per weeks most weeks of the year. It maintains the 7.2 miles of the A.T. from Pennsylvania 225 down to the bridge across the Susquehanna River at Duncannon.

CUMBERLAND VALLEY APPALACHIAN TRAIL CLUB

P.O. Box 395
Boiling Springs, PA 17007
www.cvat club.org
The Cumberland Valley Appalachian Trail Club (CVATC) builds, maintains, and manages 17.3 miles of the A.T. in the Cumberland Valley of central Pennsylvania, from Darlington Shelter to Center Point Knob.

MOUNTAIN CLUB OF MARYLAND

7923 Galloping Circle
Baltimore, MD 21244
contact@mcomd.org
www.mcomd.org
Founded in 1934 and the oldest hiking club in Maryland, Mountain Club of Maryland (MCM) maintains two A.T. sections in Pennsylvania: 12.6 miles south of the Susquehanna River to Darlington Shelter and 16.2 miles from Center Point Knob to Pine Grove Furnace State Park.

POTOMAC APPALACHIAN TRAIL CLUB

118 Park Street, S.E.
Vienna, VA 22180-4609
(703) 242-0315
www.patc.net
Founded in 1927, the Potomac Appalachian Trail Club (PATC) is based in northern Virginia outside Washington, D.C., and maintains 239.7 miles of the A.T. from Pine Grove Furnace State Park in Pennsylvania to Rockfish Gap near I-64 at Waynesboro, Virginia.

OLD DOMINION APPALACHIAN TRAIL CLUB

P.O. Box 25283
Richmond, VA 23260
www.odatc.net
The Old Dominion Appalachian Trail Club maintains 19.1 miles of the A.T. from Rockfish Gap at the southern end of Shenandoah National Park (near I-64) to Reeds Gap at Virginia 664.

TIDEWATER APPALACHIAN TRAIL CLUB

president@tidewateratc.com
www.tidewateratc.com
The Tidewater Appalachian Trail Club's primary purpose is to maintain a 10.6-mile section of the A.T. from Reeds Gap to the Tye River.

NATURAL BRIDGE APPALACHIAN TRAIL CLUB

president@nbatc.org
www.nbatc.org
Founded in 1930, the Natural Bridge Appalachian Trail Club (NBATC) now maintains 90.5 miles of the A.T. in Nelson, Amherst, Rockbridge, Botetourt, and Bedford counties, from the Tye River near Virginia 56 to Black Horse Gap at mile 97.7 of the Blue Ridge Parkway.

ROANOKE APPALACHIAN TRAIL CLUB

P.O. Box 12282
Roanoke, VA 24024-2282
www.ratc.org
The Roanoke Appalachian Trail Club maintains 121.4 miles of the A.T. from Black Horse Gap on the Blue Ridge Parkway south to Pine Swamp Branch Shelter and from Pearisburg at the New River south to Virginia 611 in Bland County.

OUTDOOR CLUB OF VIRGINIA TECH

Virginia Polytechnic Institute and State University
Blacksburg, VA 24060
ocvt-president@vt.edu
www.outdoor.org.vt.edu
The Outdoor Club of Virginia Tech, based in Blacksburg, maintains 27.8 miles of the A.T. divided into two sections: Pine Swamp Branch Shelter to U.S. 460 at the New River and Virginia 611 to U.S. 52 at Bland and Bastian.

PIEDMONT APPALACHIAN TRAIL HIKERS

P.O. Box 4423
Greensboro, NC 27404
www.path-at.org
Piedmont Appalachian Trail Hikers (PATH) maintains 64.1 miles of the A.T. in Virginia from U.S. 52 near Bland and Bastian to the South Fork of the Holston River at Virginia 670.

MOUNT ROGERS APPALACHIAN TRAIL CLUB

P.O. Box 789
Damascus, VA 24236-0789
mratcpresident@gmail.com
www.mratc.org
The Mount Rogers Appalachian Trail Club maintains 55.9 miles of the A.T. from Virginia 670 to the town of Damascus, Virginia, near the Tennessee line.

TENNESSEE EASTMAN HIKING AND CANOEING CLUB

P.O. Box 511
Kingsport, TN 37662
atchair@tehcc.org
www.tehcc.org
The Tennessee Eastman Hiking and Canoeing Club (TEHCC) maintains 136.1 miles of the A.T. between Damascus, Virginia, and U.S. 19W at Spivey Gap on the North Carolina / Tennessee border, about 12 miles south of Erwin, Tennessee.

CAROLINA MOUNTAIN CLUB

P.O. Box 68
Asheville, NC 28802
president@carolinamtnclub.org
www.carolinamtnclub.org
The Carolina Mountain Club (CMC) maintains 92.7 miles of the A.T. from Spivey Gap to Davenport Gap, also the Tennessee border, at I-40 along the eastern end of the Great Smoky Mountains National Park.

SMOKY MOUNTAINS HIKING CLUB

P.O. Box 1451
Knoxville, TN 37901
www.smhclub.org
The Appalachian Trail Maintainers Committee of Smoky Mountains Hiking Club (SMHC) maintains 101 miles of the A.T. from Davenport Gap, through the Great Smoky Mountains National Park, to the community of Wesser, North Carolina, on the Nantahala River.

NANTAHALA HIKING CLUB

173 Carl Slagle Road
Franklin, NC 28734
www.nantahalahikingclub.org
The Nantahala Hiking Club (NHC) maintains 58.5 miles of the A.T. from the Nantahala River at Wesser along U.S. 19 / 74 to Bly Gap just north of the Georgia border.

GEORGIA APPALACHIAN TRAIL CLUB

P.O. Box 654
Atlanta, GA 30301
(404) 634-6495
president@georgia-atclub.org
www.georgia-atclub.org
The Georgia Appalachian Trail Club maintains the southernmost 78.6 miles of the A.T. from Bly Gap just north of the North Carolina line to Springer Mountain in Georgia, plus the 8.8-mile approach trail from Amicalola Falls State Park.

Sources

The text in this book draws primarily on the holdings of the Appalachian Trail Conservancy archives. It also relies in significant ways on the following:

Anderson, Larry. *Benton MacKaye: Conservationist, Planner, and Creator of the Appalachian Trail.* Baltimore: The Johns Hopkins University Press, 2002.

Georgia Appalachian Trail Club, Inc. *Friendships of the Trail: The History of the Georgia Appalachian Trail Club, 1930–1980.* Marietta: Cherokee Publishing Company, 1995.

Luxenberg, Larry. *Walking the Appalachian Trail.* Mechanicsburg: Stackpole Books, 1994.

Hare, James R., ed. *Hiking the Appalachian Trail,* volumes one and two. Emmaus: Rodale Press, Inc., 1975.

Bates, David. *Breaking Trail in the Central Appalachians.* Washington: The Potomac Appalachian Trail Club, 1987.

Field, David B. *Images of America: Along Maine's Appalachian Trail.* Charleston: Arcadia Publishing, 2011.

The most comprehensive Appalachian Trail bibliography can be found on Linda Patton's Books for Hikers Internet site, www.booksforhikers.com.

Photography Credits

First published in the United States of America in 2012
by Rizzoli International Publications, Inc. • 300 Park Avenue South • New York, NY 10010 • www.rizzoliusa.com

© 2012 Appalachian Trail Conservancy • P.O. Box 807, Harpers Ferry, West Virginia 25425
Foreword © 2012 Bill Bryson

Project Editor: Candice Fehrman • Text: Brian B. King, Appalachian Trail Conservancy • Book Design: Susi Oberhelman • Map Illustrations: James Daley

APPALACHIAN TRAIL
C O N S E R V A N C Y®
www.appalachiantrail.org

2013 2014 2015 2016 / 10 9 8 7 6 5 4 3 2

Printed in China • ISBN-13: 978-0-8478-3903-2 • Library of Congress Catalog Control Number: 2012931970

p. 1: Road crossing in southern Pennsylvania • pp. 2–3: McAfee Knob near Catawba, Virginia • pp. 4–5: Jane Bald, North Carolina–Tennessee border
pp. 6–7: Moose grazes in bog south of Baxter State Park, Maine • pp. 334–335: Great Gulf Wilderness below Mount Washington, New Hampshire